D0513071

24HR
TRENCH

A DAY IN THE LIFE
OF A FRONTLINE TOMMY

BOURNEMOUTH

410064944

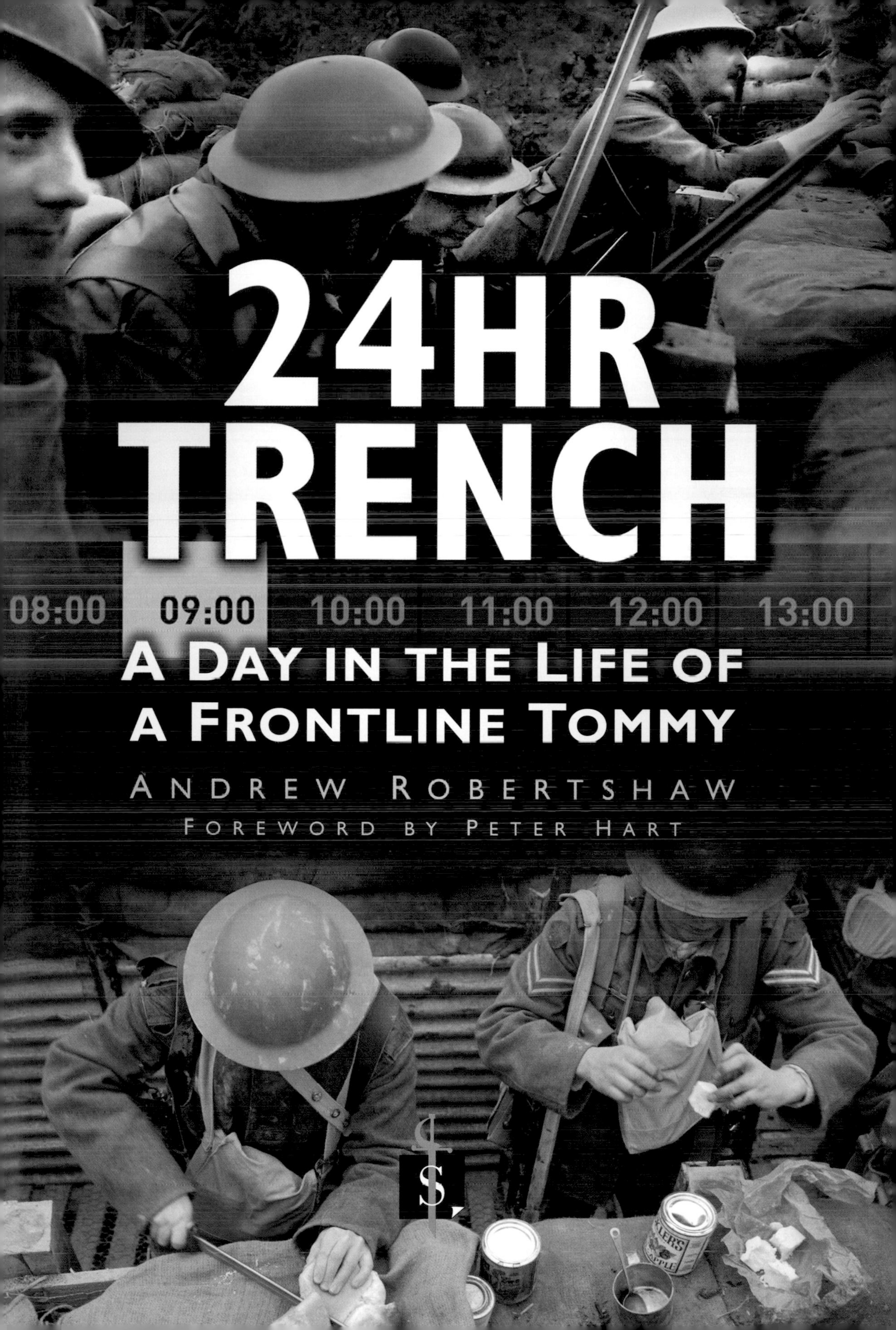

24HR
TRENCH
08:00 09:00 10:00 11:00 12:00 13:00
A DAY IN THE LIFE OF
A FRONTLINE TOMMY
ANDREW ROBERTSHAW
FOREWORD BY PETER HART

First published 2012

by Spellmount, an imprint of The History Press
The Mill, Brimscombe Port
Stroud, Gloucestershire, GL5 2QG
www.thehistorypress.co.uk

© Andrew Robertshaw, 2012

The right of Andrew Robertshaw to be identified as the Author
of this work has been asserted in accordance with the
Copyrights, Designs and Patents Act 1988.

All rights reserved. No part of this book may be reprinted
or reproduced or utilised in any form or by any electronic,
mechanical or other means, now known or hereafter invented,
including photocopying and recording, or in any information
storage or retrieval system, without the permission in writing
from the Publishers.

British Library Cataloguing in Publication Data.
A catalogue record for this book is available from the British Library.

ISBN 978 0 7524 7667 4

Typesetting and origination by The History Press
Manufacturing managed by Jellyfish Print Solutions Ltd
Printed in India.

CONTENTS

ACKNOWLEDGEMENTS

The *24hr Trench* project involved a very large number of people many of whom never saw the finished trench system, as they were not there for the weekend event and photography. I am immensely grateful for their assistance, advice and, in some cases, sweat, blood and tears. Corporal S. Haines and men of 23rd Regiment Royal Logistic Corps from St David's Barracks near Bicester carried out the basic work on the trench. Teams of various sizes made up from the following volunteers carried out the rest of the work: Martin Stiles, Steve Roberts, Lesley Wood, Anthony Roberts, Ian Wedge, Mark Khan, Pete Birkett, Max Birkett, Steve Wisdom and Dr David Kenyon. Many of the same people also provided the back-up team for the photography and some spent the night under the stars. The cook for the weekend was Diane Carpenter. There can have been few places on the Western Front in the Great War where the menu included both a vegetarian and vegan option!

The soldiers in the trench were Neil McGurk, Stephen Wisdom, Jonathan Keeling, Paul Harding, Mark Griffin (who also provided the special effects), Pete Birkett, Max Birkett, Ian Wedge, Richard Townsley, Alex Sotheran, Justin Russell, Vince Scopes, Lewis Scopes and Richard Bass. The German sniper was Martin Stiles.

Richard Ingram was a 'behind the scenes' influence providing a great deal of useful advice and a few items required for the trench. Another office-based contributor was Natalie Hill who in between work as a volunteer at the Royal Logistic Corps Museum typed text, emailed images and taught me how to use 'Dropbox'. The sniper items used were provided by Dr Roger Payne. I am immensely grateful for his support in adding a little more very expensive detail to the project.

Phil Erswell who runs PaGe Images took the majority of the photographs. He found himself pitched into 1917 and ended up conducting his longest and coldest shoot in changing light conditions whilst trying to avoid catching glimpses of the twenty-first century. Without his imagination and skill, the whole project could have been a failure.

To put the trench into context Bob Moulder did the superb drawings and even came to the site to measure up and take photographs to ensure that his work was to scale and historically accurate.

A number of suppliers contributed to the project including P.J. Judd Landscapes of East Grinstead who provided free railway sleepers and the Timberstore near Crawley which provided a great deal of inexpensive and some free timber. A good amount of the replica uniform and military equipment was provided by Richard Knight of Khaki on Campaign and the many labels and replica printed material was produced by Geoff Carefoot who runs Tommy's Pack Fillers. A specialist supplier and one whose products were very welcome by the troops was Joyce Meader who runs Historic Knit. She is a historical military hand knitter and collector of historical military printed knitting patterns.

Finally I would like to thank my wife for putting up with large numbers of people walking mud into the house whilst we demanded endless tea, coffee and hot meals. For more than six months she became a 'trench widow' with a washing machine full of muddy clothes and a garden filled with trench boards, pumps and hurdles. I am lucky to have a partner prepared to put up with my obsession with the Great War, especially when I bring it so close to home.

FOREWORD

The great battles will always be a source of fascination to the military historian. There is just so much to argue about. Strategy, tactics, the competence – or otherwise – of the generals, the twists and turns of fate. These are all grist to the mill. Yet Andrew Robertshaw has grasped the fundamental fascination of the day-to-day routine of the ordinary British soldier in the trenches. Not in battle going over the top, surrounded by bursting shells, flensing shrapnel and torrents of machine-gun bullets, but more often than not just the matter of going about their daily routine: the sort of existence experienced by millions of British soldiers throughout the war years. Details and insights once thought too mundane to be recorded in diaries, letters and books, but now as strange as life on Mars. Another world, the same planet. What was once dull now seems very strange indeed; the hardships lightly borne nearly a hundred years ago appear excessively painful to modern sensibilities.

The genius of the concept is obvious once you are immersed in this wonderful book reliving one 24-hour period for a section of men from the 1/5th King's Liverpool Regiment of the 55th Division in the Hooge sector of the Ypres Salient in January 1917.

What can we learn from this exercise? Well it doesn't take long to realise that this book is invaluable to an understanding of what life was like for our forbears in a realistic trench built without the comforting refuge of the modern health and safety standards so beloved by film and television producers. The results are amazing. I had the pleasure of interviewing nearly 200 Great War veterans for the Imperial War Museum Sound Archive back in the 1980s and I thought I knew almost everything there was to know about the daily routine. It was, after all, a key part of that oral history project: delving into their memories to look at the 'stand to', cooking and meals, sentry duty, the graft of repairing damage to the trenches, writing home to girlfriends and family, ration parties, fatigues – everything and anything we could think of. We certainly recorded and learnt a lot, but this book has brought everything sharply into focus. The combination of carefully posed photographs, diagrams, sketches and an authoritative text is an outstanding method of revealing how things actually worked in practice.

We see how a soldier was kitted out with his uniform and equipment from top to bottom. Whether it be his undergarments, the origin of the term 'belt and braces', or the arcane secrets of the '08 pattern webbing, there is plenty to learn, plenty to fascinate. I have never seen such a clear demonstration of what the men wore and how it all fitted together.

Although restricted in scale to just a couple of bays of frontline, dugouts and a section of communication trench, the '24-Hour Trench' was a still a major construction task undertaken by the men of the 23rd Pioneer Regiment, Royal Logistic Corps, and then finished off by the volunteers. This was evidently very much a learning experience: it certainly brought to mind that the Western Front involved thousands upon thousands of miles of trenches, each dug by hand, often under fire. The amount of labour involved is beyond belief.

The mysteries of the trench and trench life are then gradually revealed, not in aged black-and-white photos but in sharp, modern colour prints. Now you can really see what is happening! How do they brew their tea in those front-line trenches? What is a Tommy cooker? Does the rum ration make you drunk? Then there were the insights into how physically hard it really was. The dreadful freezing cold of stints of sentry duty; the soaking wet collapsing trenches, where mud is all around; the perils of shaving with a cut-throat razor; the daily ritual of cleaning their rifles – their 'best friend' should they have to go into action. Most evocative of all is the picture of one young soldier reading a 'letter from home' while defecating for 'King and Country' in the latrine built into the side of the communication trench: an often forgotten or sidestepped part of daily life in the trenches. The German activity is restricted to a single sniper shot, but the continual threat posed by such sniping forces all tall men to crouch down to try to ensure that their heads do not appear above the parapet for even a moment. After the evening 'stand to' there is the sheer hard graft of a night spent 'improv-ing' the trench, enlivened by a gas scare that forces everyone into their gas masks. Sleep is hard to come by. Photos acutely reveal the very real exhaustion suffered by the volunteers even in this staged re-creation.

There are many ways to learn about the Great War. The old tried and trusted methods of books and documents still have great value, while sound recordings have considerably broadened our viewpoint. Then again the recent developments in battlefield archaeology have allowed us the electric charge of excitement of seeing history emerge from the ground. But the '24-Hour Trench' re-creation, rig-orously controlled to ensure all possible realism, has brought the whole thing to life in a unique fashion. It ties everything together, unifying our picture so that we can really get to grips with the nitty-gritty of life in the trenches. We owe a debt to Andrew Robertshaw and his intrepid team of volunteers.

Peter Hart

AUTHOR'S NOTE

Having spent seven years as a classroom teacher and twenty-two years at the National Army Museum in Chelsea, I estimate that I have taught more than half a million young people about the Western Front in the Great War. In that time, I have tried to describe the routine of trench life, rather than simply barrages, going over the top and endless war poetry. Sadly, the nature of the curriculum and the focus of interest has always been the day of battle rather than the ordinary tour in the frontline. My grandfather served between 1916 and 1918. In this time he was involved in the closing days of the Battle of the Somme, was in reserve during the Battle of Arras, in the frontline for the major German attack of spring 1918 and was in action during the Allied '100 Days' offensive. During that time, he was 'in action' for no more than a few days, was wounded three times and came home once, wounded. By far the majority of his time was spent alternating between weeks in 'the line', 'in reserve' and 'resting'. An account of his career, which focused on his few days in battle, may emphasise what we find interesting today, but it is not typical of his experience or that of his comrades.

One early idea I had with the '24-Hour Trench' concept was to use a replica trench in a museum as a backdrop on to which an audio-visual display could be projected. The plan would be to speed up reality to compress the typical trench day into something that a museum audience would be happy to watch. However, every time the project was discussed in a gallery planning group, someone would suggest 'just' adding in some shellfire, a gas attack or a trench raid to make the experience 'more typical'. My response that this would, if anything, make the whole thing less typical was ignored and the project was quietly abandoned. This resulted in my decision to turn the project into a book covering just 24 hours in a real trench, in a real location at some point in the war. The advantage of a book is that I had complete control of the content and that the readers could take their time to absorb the detail. In addition, by being based on real events, it would not simply be another 'typical' book about the Great War.

To make the book as accurate as possible required a great deal of research and I was very fortunate that my colleague Steve Roberts was able to use his time at the National Archives, Kew, to look at various war diaries for units relevant to my chosen sector of the line – Hooge near Ypres. One disappointment for me as a Yorkshireman was the discovery that the most appropriate division in the line was recruited in Lancashire. However, historical accuracy forbade me from tinkering with the facts. The period in which the division held the line between Wieltje to Railway Wood in the spring of 1917 is described in the divisional history as follows:

During the first few months the sector was might be called a 'quiet' sector. Both the enemy and ourselves were tired after the strenuous work of the Somme and required, and obtained, rest.

The Story of the 55th (West Lancashire) Division, Rev. J.O. Coop, Liverpool,
1919, p. 46

By being strictly authentic, I was also able to make a key point about the experience of the frontline. One battalion of around 800 men in the division in question suffered two casualties during their tour of frontline duty. One man suffered head injuries when he fell down a well in the dark and another cut himself so badly on corrugated iron that he was medically evacuated and the nature of his injury mentioned in the War Diary. In other words, during nearly four days of frontline service in one of the most disputed areas of the British-held sector of the Western Front despite shelling, snipers, machine guns and mortars, no one was injured sufficiently badly by enemy fire to be treated for their wounds. In the same period, no one was killed! It would always be possible to argue that this was exceptional, the evidence indicates otherwise, but the key fact is that this is what happened. This meant that I felt confident that I could take one day out of a tour of duty in the frontline for an infantry unit, show the full routine in the 24 hours and miss out heavy shelling, mass casualties or any other cliché of movies and still be historically accurate.

The final question was how many men to portray as my 'typical unit'. By 1917, a platoon of around thirty-six soldiers was the main tactical sub-unit of the British Army. I was daunted by the feeding and housing of this number of soldiers even if they were all volunteers and was aware that I would need rather more trench to house them than I had space to build. The solution was to represent the smallest sub-unit 'The Section'. This consisted of ten or a dozen men and there were four within each platoon. According to the pencilled additions to my copy of the *Training Manual S.S.143, Instruction for The Training of Platoons For Offensive Action, 1917*, No.1 Section was equipped with one or more Lewis machine guns, No.2 Section consisted of bombers armed with rifles but trained to throw hand grenades and No.4 Section was armed with rifles equipped with dischargers that could fire grenades to long distance. These were all specialists. The most 'ordinary' section was No.3, the riflemen. This is not quite correct, as the men in this section were the best shots, snipers and bayonet fighters. However, to make my section representative of the ordinary soldier it was ideal. All I had to do was to take just over a dozen volunteers, clothe, equip and arm them historically accurately for 1917, then put them in a replica trench system under conditions as close to 'the real' experience as possible for just over 24 hours so they could be photographed. When I first thought about the idea, it did seem ambitious. It did not get easier.

A WORLD ENTRENCHED

Since the end of the Great War in November 1918, trenches and trench warfare have defined our understanding of the conflict. It is easy to forget that the war began in August 1914 as one of manoeuvre, not trenches and barbed wire. The war began with the vast German right hook of the Schlieffen Plan, which aimed to capture Paris and force France to surrender as it had done in 1870. While this was going on French troops advanced in the south in an attempt to recapture the provinces of Alsace and Lorraine ceded to Prussia as penalty for the same defeat. With these vast conscript armies in movement, the British Expeditionary Force (BEF) marched from railheads in France in defence of Belgian neutrality. The French attack, Plan XVII, was a failure and the British found themselves in a fighting retreat from the Belgian town of Mons.

This retreat continued almost to the gates of Paris, 150 miles (240km) distance, by which time the German Army was virtually exhausted. The Battle of the Marne that followed saw the German invaders on the defensive and under increasing Allied pressure. Despite attempts by both armies to outflank the other and achieve total victory, the 'race to the sea' created a situation by early November in which the contending armies faced one another on a front from Switzerland to the North Sea. Germany was now at war on two fronts: East and West. Having failed to deliver the hoped-for knock-out blow to France, the Russian Army was now mobilised and threatening Prussia and the German capital, Berlin. The only way in which the German Army could deal with both threats was to go on to the defensive – relying on a well-entrenched garrison in the West to hold off the combined French, British and Belgian forces, while her troops in the East attempted to defeat the Russians. Under these circumstances, the Germans could select the most easily defensive positions and use local resources to 'dig in'. They were well aware that the only way that the Allies could recapture the lost ground in Belgium and northern France would be by mounting costly attacks on the German defences. Effectively the Allies could only win by attacking, while the Germans could stay on the defensive, knowing that they held a critical advantage of captured territory. Throughout the war the high command of both sides said that trench warfare was merely a 'phase' in the conflict and that it was inevitable that open warfare would resume at some point. This occurred, to some extent, in the spring of 1917 when the Germans withdrew to their previously constructed line of defences known to the Allies as the 'Hindenburg Line'. Then again from early August 1918, when during the '100 Days' the Allies mounted an all-out offensive on the Western Front. Although the advances made by the Allies were not in the same league as later fully mechanised warfare, there was little opportunity to dig in during the 'Advance to Victory'. The Armistice of 11 November terminated the fighting in a secession of hostilities before the Allies could invade Germany as many had hoped.

Under the circumstances of late 1914, the Germans could dictate the nature of the trench warfare that was to follow. Not only could they give up ground that they considered to be of limited military advantage, something the Allies could not consider because of the implications of being seen to hand 'friendly' ground to the enemy, they were also able to exploit the natural and industrial resources of the occupied territories. In many cases, the Germans took up position first and were able to begin to dig in before their opponents came in too close a proximity to their new lines. Elsewhere there was no choice but to dig in close to their opponents, with both sides using entrenching tools to get below ground as quickly as possible. Speed was critically important in daylight when men who were not rapid enough would become victim to enemy weapons. Not surprisingly, both sides tried to use the hours of darkness to establish or improve their positions and the nocturnal nature of trench warfare would be a feature of the rest of the war. Whenever the trenches were dug, they were not simple random holes in the landscape. It was vital that trenches had a 'Field of Fire' so that the men occupying the system could target the opposing trenches or attacking enemy soldiers in no-man's-land. Equally critical was protection because a trench that was overlooked by the enemy on higher ground, or situated on a hill top so that the garrison could be seen against the sky line, were to be avoided. If possible, the trench would be concealed in some way using existing hedges, banks, cuttings or woodland. Otherwise these features could be marked on maps, making the trench more easily targeted by artillery fire. Finally, a good trench would be sited so that men in other friendly positions could assist the garrison with supporting fire. These factors all determined the layout and nature of trenches, but it was impossible to achieve perfect conditions so all real trenches were a compromise to some extent.

The final factor to take into account was geology. On the Somme, chalk is found below the surface at depths that range from a few metres to a few centimetres. This was good news for the occupants of a trench as whereas, according to the official manual, it took 40in (101cm) of earth to stop a bullet, 15in (38cm) of chalk could do the same. Chalk also meant that water drained away freely even if the topsoil could turn into mud very easily with a little rain. Once the trenches extended into the chalk, it required pickaxes and hard labour to make any impression on the layer. One additional problem was concealment and the chalk thrown up as spoil indicated the line of the trenches to any observer. Even today, nearly 100 years later, chalk marks can be seen after fresh ploughing to indicate the position of long-filled-in trenches. Concealing spoil from the excavating of dugouts was vitally important. If chalk waste was dumped in an area where there had been little previously it would indicate to the enemy that mining or dugout construction was taking place. The result could be shelling or, worse still, a raid to find out what was happening. The good news about working in chalk was that it required little support from timbering and it was possible to excavate very deep quite quickly. By midway through the war and with the size of shells increasing, this depth meant safety for dugout occupants. It was estimated that it took 20ft (6m) of chalk to make a dugout shell proof compared to more than 30ft (9m) of clay.

Further north, the British trench lines ran through areas with less chalk and great amounts of clay and a higher water table. Here it was necessary not to dig the trenches down, but to build them up using earth from behind and in front of the 'command trench'. This produced a dry, well-drained trench, but one that involved a vast amount of labour and one that did not offer the protection of a conventional system. Most problematic was the firing position created for the garrison. As the men were firing whilst standing above natural ground level it was difficult to hit targets close to the trench in the area of 'Dead Ground', a factor that could be exploited by an attacker. As techniques of trench construction improved command trenches were increasingly less popular. They were replaced by conventional trenches provided with trench boards, sumps and pumps designed to remove water from the trenches and counter the problem of 'trench foot' caused by loss of circulation in men who stood for too long in

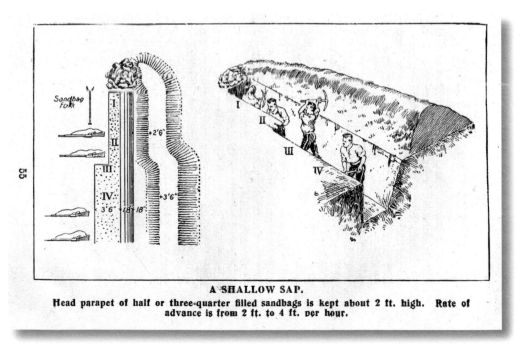

A SHALLOW SAP.
Head parapet of half or three-quarter filled sandbags is kept about 2 ft. high. Rate of advance is from 2 ft. to 4 ft. per hour.

Early trenches were very primitive and owed more to siege warfare than conditions on the Western Front.

cold, wet trenches. The big problem with wet and clay areas was the amount of material required to reinforce the trenches. Chalk trenches will stand with an almost vertical cut for months on end suffering more from frost than rain or side pressure. Trenches dug into clay may start with a vertical side but a combination of rain, frost, hot weather and the weight of the material will result in inevitable collapse unless the sides are revetted (fitted with sloping structures to secure the area, from the French to re-clothe/re-cover). To make this situation worse clay is virtually the least resistant material, generally used to fill sandbags or construct defences. On average, it took 80in (202cm) of clay to stop a bullet, twice that of ordinary earth and five times more than chalk. This meant that the mass of the structure, the thickness of the sandbag parapet and even head cover had to be so much greater to provide the same level of protection.

The final problem faced by anyone who attempted to 'dig in' in an area with clay geology was the question of dugouts. Although it was possible to dig shallow cut and cover shelters virtually anywhere, provided they were pumped dry on a regular basis, digging deeper brought two problems. The first was flooding and the second, potential catastrophic collapse. One of the big advantages offered to the German defenders of the Ypres Salient they occupied was that they could dig in using the relatively well-drained geology of the ridge to remain safe and dry. For the British, confined to the low ground with poor geology and a high water table, building safe shelters and avoiding flooding were a constant problem. These problems would also be a feature of the *24hr Trench* project, creating rather more authentic conditions than we had planned.

This is what the German Army imagined would happen in 1914: a victorious march on Paris and the war over before Christmas. Andrew Robertshaw Collection.

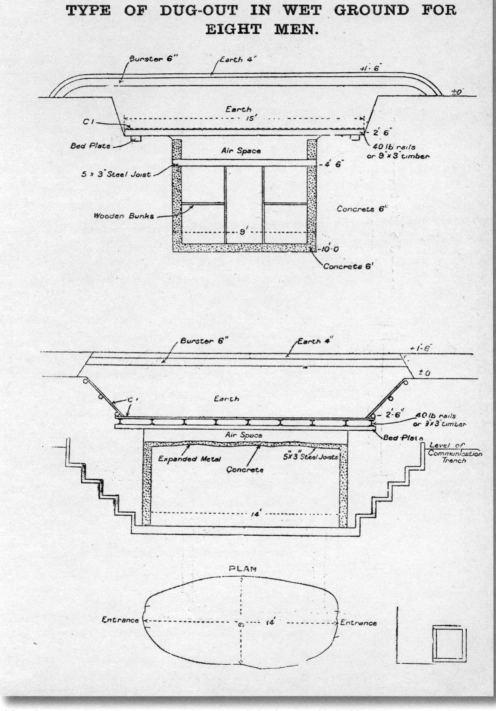

TYPE OF DUG-OUT IN WET GROUND FOR EIGHT MEN.

Although apparently simple, the amount of earth needed to be moved to build even a shallow dugout is formidable.

Plate 9.

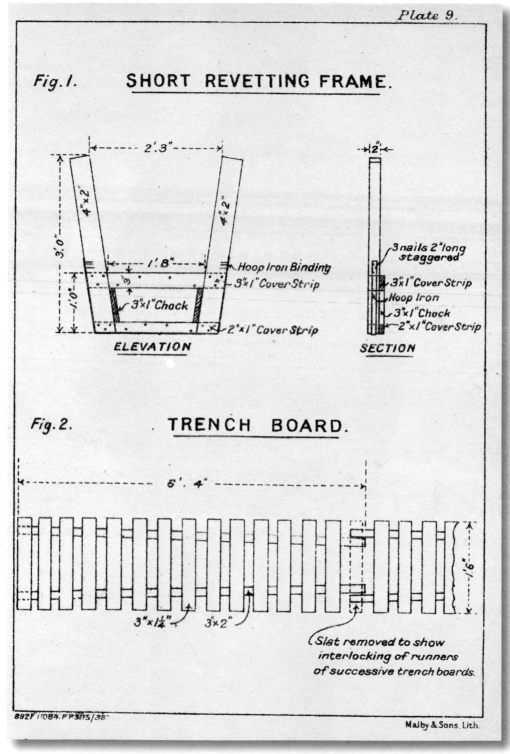

Fig.1. **SHORT REVETTING FRAME.**

2'.3"

4"×2" 4"×2"

3'.0"

1'.8"

Hoop Iron Binding

3"×1" Cover Strip

1'.0"

3"×1"Chock

2"×1" Cover Strip

ELEVATION

2"

3 nails 2"long staggered

3"×1"Cover Strip

Hoop Iron

3"×1"Chock

2"×1"CoverStrip

SECTION

Fig.2. **TRENCH BOARD.**

5'. 4"

1'.6"

3"×1¼"   3"×2"

Slat removed to show interlocking of runners of successive trench boards.

Malby & Sons Lith.

The amount of timber used to build and support trenches is far greater than one would assume. The frames and boards both prevent the structure from collapsing and keep the user's feet out of the mud. From: *Manual of Field Works (All Arms)*, 1921.

THE TYPICAL SOLDIER

It has become increasingly a feature of any description of a British soldier in the Great War to describe him as 'young'; many were. The official age for service overseas was 19 and although a large number of young men lied about their age and served 'under age', the majority were considerably older. In January 1916, the Military Service Act was introduced. Under the act every British male who was over the age of 19 but not yet 41 and was unmarried or a widower without dependants or children was eligible to be conscripted. Men who were prepared to re-enlist were already being accepted up to the age of 45 and this upper age eventually rose to over 50. In the Second World War, the maximum age for conscription or volunteering for the armed forces was set at 40 years of age. This was considerably younger than the previous war and one effect was to ensure that the generation of men who had served in the Great War were in the Home Guard rather than overseas. The consequence of this decision was to deny a large number of experienced men a 'second chance' of military service, but also to reduce the average age of Second World War servicemen compared with the Great War. A rather rough comparison indicates that men who served in the Great War army had an average age of 27 whilst those in the Second World War army were around 24 years old.

The unit chosen for our reconstruction, the 55th Division in 1917, was largely made up from members of the Territorial Force with pre-war experience. These men had been joined by some wartime volunteers and some conscripts, although the Territorial battalions did not like to see their volunteer status watered down in this way. As conscripts could not be under 19 and the pre-war Territorials had already seen three years' service (although there would be a few young soldiers in the ranks), the majority would be in their mid to late twenties.

By the standards of the time they were also quite well educated. Most of the men in the ranks would have left school around the age of 13 or 14 years, although a few would have attended grammar schools for longer. Others would have then had periods of technical training, whilst the majority would have been apprenticed for six or seven years. Most completed their apprenticeship at around the age of 21 and many of the volunteers for the Territorials were this age. Unlike the Regular Army that took recruits because they had no other employment, the Territorial Force could afford to be quite selective. Most Territorials had paid employment and volunteered because service offered additional income, challenges not provided by civilian life and a change of routine. Nights in Drill Halls, weekend camps and longer periods under canvas every summer were part of a social life linked to service and there was always the satisfaction of doing 'one's bit'. Because of the social status enjoyed by the Territorials, the rank structure often mirrored the community from which the unit had been recruited. Officers tended to be managers or business owners, senior NCOs to be qualified members of staff from businesses which could be as varied as heavy industry or engineering or dock work. The 'rank and file' tended to share a similar background and every battalion would recruit from a small community and its local employers. Quite a few men volunteered in order to help improve their standing with an employer, especially if he was sympathetic to the idea of Territorial service, whilst serving under the command of your boss or manager could be seen as helping promotion.

Whatever your reason for being a 'Saturday Night Soldier', as they were commonly called, it provided the critical skill which would be vitally important in August 1914: military training. At the time of the outbreak of war every nation in Europe, including Switzerland, had some system of conscription. Men when they became 20 were chosen by ballot for a period of regular military service, which was followed by successive periods with reserve and home guard forces. The result was that the armies of Britain's allies and enemies numbered in millions. However, Britain with its fear of standing armies relied on a volunteer army, which could produce just 247,500 Regular soldiers backed up by 200,000 Reservists. In these circumstances the existence of the Territorial force was vital, because although Kitchener's appeal for volunteers produced tens of thousands of eager volunteers in late 1914 and early 1915, these men were all untrained. In early 1916 the commander of the British Expeditionary Force, Sir Douglas Haig, was forced to remind the prime minister that despite the number of men in uniform he did not have an army under his command, he 'had an army in training'. This was not the case with the Territorials, many of whom had years of experience in uniform and under arms. Although the Territorials did not get the most modern weapons and equipment at the same time as the Regulars, their training followed a similar pattern and they shared many training areas and facilities with their 'full-time' comrades. Importantly the Territorial associations had private funding to purchase new equipment and when the Regular infantry was provided with modern woven webbing equipment the Territorials ensured that their men received comparable equipment. By the eve of war, it was largely his cap badge and details of weapons and equipment that betrayed that a 'Terrier' was not a Regular, although the 'full-time soldier' could always criticise aspects of his drill and turn out.

On the outbreak of war, the Regulars and Reservists were mobilised and sent to the front. They were soon followed first by Territorial battalions and then complete Territorial divisions for service either in the far-flung corners of the Empire or the Western Front. As the members of the Territorial Force had volunteered purely for home defence they had to be individually prepared to take the 'Imperial Service Obligation' which allowed them to be sent overseas. In most cases whole units volunteered en bloc and only a few refused to take the oath.

The 55th Division was formed in France in January 1916 and served with distinction on the Somme before being moved to the Ypres Salient in October. By the winter of 1916/17, the majority of men in the ranks knew their business. Unlike Kitchener's New Army divisions, formed from eager but under-trained and inexperienced volunteers from 1914, the men in the 55th would have considered themselves professionals. They were armed and equipped largely identically to the Regulars and they had demonstrated in early actions and during the long battle on the Somme that they were not second rate. The lessons of that long battle of attrition were being learned during the autumn of 1916 and by early in 1917 new tactics and methods of using weapons were being taught. Throughout December 1916 and into January 1917 elements of the 55th Division held the frontline, or reserve line in rotation, or were held in reserve in Ypres. The 1/5th King's Liverpool Regiment took over the trenches at Railway Wood on 19 December. They held the line until the evening of the 22nd when they were relieved by the 1/6th Liverpool Regiment and moved into billets in Ypres. For the next two days, the battalion provided working parties, but on the 25th the battalion was excused duties and enjoyed Christmas festivities. On the 26th, the battalion was employed on working parties and on the night of the 27th relieved the 6th Battalion in the frontline. They were still holding this position on New Year's Eve. The winter of 1916 to 1917 was one of the coldest on record and the periods in the line must have stretched the soldiers' endurance to its limits. According to the War Diary, in the period 19 to 22 December 1916, the 5th Battalion suffered four men wounded, two men killed and six men sick, these latter being largely the result of intense cold and exposure.

It would be difficult to describe a typical soldier in the 1/5th King's but a composite based on a couple of real soldiers will indicate the type of men they were.

Arthur Ruffler was born in Birkenhead in July 1892 and worked as a shipping clerk in Liverpool. Arthur enlisted into the Territorials shortly after it was created in 1908 and had six years of pre-war training before war was declared. He married aged 22, by coincidence, shortly before war was declared, to the daughter of a neighbour living near his family home. On the declaration of war, he took the Imperial Obligation and after intensive training in the United Kingdom went to France in February 1915. By early 1917, he was veteran of fighting both at Festubert in May 1915 and then holding the line south of Arras in spring 1916. By the time the division went into action on the Somme in early September, Arthur was a lance corporal and a bomber. By January 1917, aged 25, he was serving as the corporal in charge of a section of men he knew well. One had previously worked in his office in Liverpool as the tea boy, three had been with him in the Territorials and of the others only two had not seen action before. Even if they did not necessarily support the same football team, the men had a great deal in common. The bond of comradeship and friendship was as important as training and equipment in the forthcoming time 'up the line'.

TRENCH KIT

From the perspective of very nearly 100 years, it is easy to see the uniform and equipment of the British soldier of the Great War as old fashioned and impractical even when it was new. By comparison with modern kit the whole appearance is far from smart, is shapeless and lacks the sophistication of layered ballistic protection or disruptive camouflage. However, when first issued the uniform and equipment of the British soldier in the Great War was the most well designed and practical of any European army. Based on a number of manuals and some sets of personal accounts from soldiers who served in the trenches, I assembled a full set of real and replica uniform, protective and personal equipment, weapons and rations. It was noticeable that all of this kit would fit into a large crate, but that it was almost impossible for one person to lift it up. A number of accounts mention that the greatcoat was not popular in the trenches so I replaced this with a leather jerkin which features in many photographs of men at this stage in the war. The total weight, allowing for a full water bottle of 2 pints (1 litre) and 200 rifle rounds is just over 70lb (32kg). An average modern adult male weighs about 125lb (84kg), so this load represents more than a third of his body weight. One notable feature of this weight is that it is virtually the same as the load carried by a Roman soldier or medieval knight. However, the weather could make things worse, as the clothing is linen and wool, and the equipment cotton webbing, all of which will absorb moisture. A wet soldier would be carrying far more weight.

This is the full uniform, equipment and weapons of a British soldier in early 1917.

1 What today is called the 'base layer' consisted in the Great War of a pair of woollen drawers or 'Long Johns', a woollen vest and a pair of socks. The drawers were not elasticised and an adjustment tape was fitted in the small of the back in order to make them fit better to the wearer's shape. The underwear was issued by the quartermaster although socks and other knitted items were a popular present to receive from home. Woollen undergarments would be replaced with cotton in summer.

2 The collarless shirt was the next garment. Made from grey flannel it opened only to the chest and had to be put on over the head. As only officers were allowed to wear a collar and tie, other ranks' shirts were not designed to be fitted with a collar. Many men preferred to wear their own civilian shirts when they knew they were not going to be inspected.

3 The 1902 Pattern Service Dress trousers were made from the same Drab (Khaki) material as the tunic and fitted with two side pockets. They were designed to be roomy and worn high on the body. One cartoon of the Great War shows a young soldier wearing a pair of somewhat over-sized issue trousers; asked by the quartermaster whether they are a good fit, his response is that they are 'a bit tight round the arm pits'. With no real waist, the trousers remained in position only because the wearer used braces (suspenders), which fastened to metal buttons in the lining of the trousers. Note that leather tabs on the braces pass through the loops on the soldier's drawers so that the shirt is worn inside the underpants. One reason for this is to ensure that the underwear did not fall down inside the trousers. It also meant that when the soldier took his trousers down for a 'call of nature' the undergarments did not fall on to the floor or a muddy latrine. However, if worn without braces the trousers would tend to fall down.

4 All soldiers were, in theory, issued with a jackknife. This large folding knife had a blade, 'Marlin spike' for making holes in leather kit, tins or equipment, plus a useful, if cumbersome, tin opener. To avoid loss the knife was fitted with a copper swivel through which a lanyard could be looped. With the lanyard worn round the waist, the knife could be dropped into a pocket to keep it safe.

5 Although the issue 1903 Pattern belt may appear redundant for a man wearing braces, it was vital if he was to do any work. The braces were made from un-elasticised fabric and buttoned directly to the trousers.

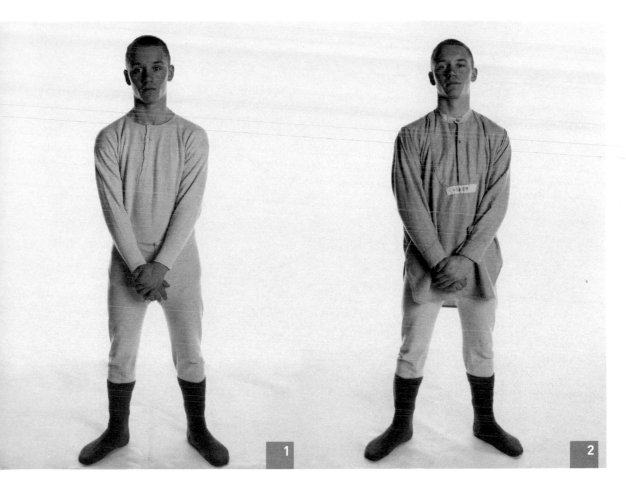

1. The soldier in his 'base layer' of underwear and socks. Note the double pair of loops formed from tape on both sides of the drawers.

2. The shirt was designed to be very long and even without a pair of pants would preserve the soldier's dignity. Note the last five digits of the soldier's regimental number stamped on the white tape.

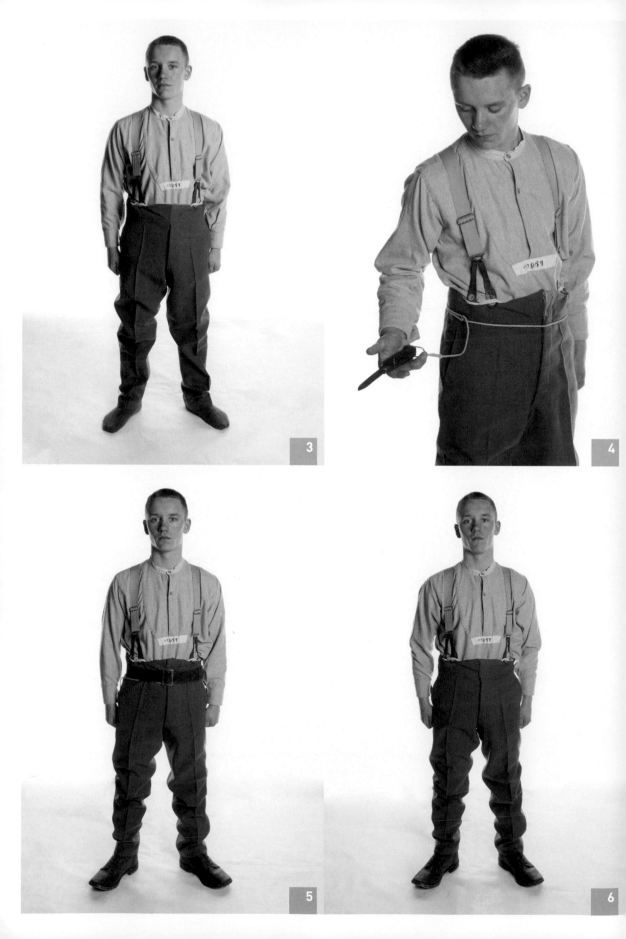

3. Service Dress trousers were intended to be worn on exercise and campaign and lacked decoration. They were, however, based on contemporary civilian fashion and were comfortable and hard wearing.

4. Despite the lethal-looking blade the jackknife was the Swiss Army knife for the Great War British soldier. It was as likely to be used to cut up cheese, open a parcel or safely pry open the split pin in a grenade.

5. The leather '03 Pattern belt was normally worn as issued but many soldiers decorated their belts with cap badge souvenirs and these are very collectable today.

6. British other ranks were issued with an ankle boot with steels at the toe and heel plus hob nails to improve grip and extend the wearing life of the boot. The boots here are of the B5 pattern, which appeared in 1916.

7. It was important for a soldier to have neat puttees. Fashion dictated that the trousers were to be 'bloused' over the top of these to hide the fastening tape and make a smart appearance. Puttees that were loose or came undone on the march would mark a man out for punishment.

8. The ID tags are worn on a glazed string around the neck with the red disc below the other and a separate string loop. Despite rumours to the contrary, the material from which the tags are made can burn and will rot.

9. This khaki sleeveless jumper is a typical knitted garment sent to a man in the trenches. This example has been made to one of the many thousands of patterns issued in magazines at the time.

If a man bent over to work whilst digging or working below waist height, there was a very good chance that one or more buttons at the back would simply pop off. If this happened his trousers would gently fall down. However, if the soldier 'shrugged' his braces off his shoulders and maintained his trousers with a belt this would not happen. This method of working gives us the expression 'Belt and Braces' which we still use today without any idea of the origins of the term.

6
7
Odd to modern eyes, puttees (with a name that is derived from the Hindustani word for bandages) were worn by British soldiers from the 1880s. Nine feet (3m) long, they were worn by the infantry, wound up the leg and fastened off with a tape just below the knee. It was important to keep the spiral even and that the end of the puttee should be the same on both legs. Certain units had rules concerning the way in which puttees should be crossed to form a pattern and this could indicate a soldier's specialism or trade. On the march, puttees supported the wearer's calves and in the trenches they protected the top of his boots from mud and damp in addition to preventing the trousers becoming torn.

8
From the outbreak of war, all servicemen were issued a single metal, later red vulcanised, fibre identification disc. On to this was stamped his surname and initials, religion, regimental number and regiment. From September 1916 a second green/grey octagonal tag was added to ensure that if the wearer was killed and one of the discs removed there would still be some means of identification.

9
To ensure that a soldier could remain warm his tunic was designed to be sufficiently large for him to wear multiple layers of clothing beneath. Here a privately knitted sleeveless jumper provides additional warmth. A whole host of knitted goods from body belts and cardigans to gloves, caps and scarves were produced for family members or simply as presents for the men at 'the front'. Sadly not all items were equally well received and some ended up as rifle covers, cleaning cloths or improvised bandages.

10
Although a soldier was issued with a helmet, when out of the line he wore a cap which, in a society in which men all wore some sort of head gear out-doors, would have been worn at all times. Early in the war, the stiffened Service Dress cap was issued to all soldiers. With the introduction of steel helmets in late 1915, the disadvantage of having a form of headgear that could not be folded up

14

15

10. Even the military falls victim to fashion and the wearing of trench caps became a subject of much debate. The belief was that wearing it flat on the head indicted the wearer's status as a new boy. If it was worn pulled right back it indicated someone who was an experienced soldier, an 'old sweat'.

11. The leather jerkin has remained an item of issued kit in the British Army from its introduction in 1915 almost until today. Once they appeared as war surplus, they were very popular from the 1950s to '80s with dustbin men.

12. The tunic was always intended to be worn over other clothing and buttoned easily despite the many layers of garments worn beneath.

13. The pay book had a stout waterproof cover and a large number of less than official pieces of paper, from letters to tickets, ended up between the pages of the AB 64.

14. The reason for the two bandages in the field dressing was to ensure that the user could treat 'a through and through' bullet wound in which the victim would have two injuries.

15. The great advantage of the '08 Webbing was its balance when worn and the fact that it could be put on as a waistcoat. In an early demonstration of its value, one of the developers of the equipment put on a fully loaded set and then walked on his hands across the room.

16. To do up the waist belt the free end is passed round the opposing buckle and pulled back to tighten round the waist. Fashion dictated that there should be no loose end but if the wearer was on a long march, the belt could be left undone for an easy march.

and stored became apparent. This led to the introduction of a soft cap commonly referred to as a 'trench cap'. This could be simply rolled up and placed in a haversack or pocket without suffering ill effects.

11 Certain items were issued to individual soldiers and became their property, hence the importance of marking kit. This did not extend to some items of protective clothing, much of which was issued on a seasonal basis. Here the soldier has received the standard leather jerkin with its woollen lining and large leather 'football' buttons. The covering of mud indicates that the previous wearer has been in the trenches. This could be worn over the uniform tunic, but if worn in this fashion it was impossible to access pockets. Worn underneath the tunic the jerkin kept the wearer both warm and dry.

12 The Service Dress tunic was made from the same 'Drab' fabric as the trousers and provided with two breast pockets, two internal pockets and two side pockets. Some examples had 'rifle patch' reinforcements at shoulder level as the tunic was largely based on civilian shooting wear. The garment was unlined and could absorb moisture very readily. However, being made from wool, the fabric dries rapidly and is surprisingly warm and comfortable. The brass 'shoulder titles', which in this instance simply say 'King's', worn on both epaulets indicated the wearer's regiment. A green strip of felt is worn between the wearer's shoulder blades as the battalion's 'battle insignia'. A different colour and shape was worn by each unit in the division.

13 Although soldiers were not instructed in which pocket their personal items should be put, one important document, the Army Book 64 or 'pay book', was meant to be in the left breast pocket. This book contained information about the soldier's qualifications, pay, medical history and personal will. Loss of the book was a punishable offence.

14 It was vitally important that if a soldier was injured in action he could give himself first aid. For this reason all soldiers were issued with a 'First Field Dressing' which consisted of two bandages in a waterproof outer wrapper. To ensure this could be found when necessary one of the features of the interior of the tunic was a small pocket in the right lower skirt of the garment. The dressing was stored here so that it was ready for him to use or, if he was incapacitated, a comrade would know where to find it.

21

22

17. Here the rear view shows the position of the haversack with mess tin buckled through its straps. Beneath this sits the entrenching tool head. On the left hip the bayonet and entrenching tool helve (handle) can be seen.

18. With the head slipped on to the helve the tool could be used to break up hard ground and move earth quite efficiently. When not required the elements could be stored away on the equipment.

19. Ammunition carried in a bandolier is not well protected from the weather or mud and normally on arrival in a position this would be checked and stored centrally. On Great War archaeological sites hundreds of full bandoliers have been uncovered, suggesting that not all this weighty ammunition reached its destination.

20. When not close to the enemy, or when there was little threat of gas attack, the respirator was worn under the left arm.

21. The respirator satchel was worn slightly open but with the mask covered to prevent this becoming soaked with rain.

22. Now virtually fully laden, the weight is taken on the shoulders and waist, but there is always space for a few more minor items and pockets bulge with everything from spare socks to boiled sweets.

15 Adopted by the British Army in 1908 the Mills '08 Pattern Web Equipment was approximately the same colour as the wearer's uniform. It was made from woven cotton that did not require constant maintenance, and it could be put on in one piece, unlike the equipment of other nations. Here the soldier has just put on the equipment with 150 rounds of ammunition, a bayonet, entrenching tool, 2 pints of water (1 litre), a set of mess tins for cooking and the contents of his haversack which include a ground sheet, rations, washing and shaving kit, and all the personal items needed for a few days in the field.

16 It had been realised that men with cold and tired hands had great difficulty in adjusting normal buckles on military equipment. The Mills pattern introduced 'tongueless buckles' in which the wearer could adjust the size of any strap or fitting by simply sliding the webbing to left or right.

17 Although the rear view demonstrated that the webbing equipment did not allow for parade-ground smartness it was easy to put on and fairly comfortable to wear. In 'battle order', the haversack worn in the centre of the back with water on the right hip and bayonet and entrenching tool handle on the opposite hip reduced the soldier's width. This was very important in tight trenches. Although it was possible to reach the entrenching tool head oneself, access to the mess tins or haversack required either the removal of the equipment or asking a comrade for help.

18 Although soldiers were supplied with specialist digging equipment when in the trenches or going into battle it was recognised that an emergency implement should be carried by the infantry. The 'pick mattock' or entrenching tool was created. It was carried in two sections ready to be assembled, although the head could be used as a simple trowel.

19 The equipment could carry up to 150 rounds of rifle ammunition in ten pouches. It was, however, clear that even this amount of ammunition may not be sufficient and soldiers going into action or on duty in the trenches would carry reserves. Here the cotton bandolier in which ammunition was issued is being used to carry an additional 100 rounds.

20 When the German Army first used gas on the Western Front in May 1916 gas masks had to be improvised. By September 1916 British scientists had developed the Small Box Respirator (SBR), a gas mask that could defend the wearer against virtually all forms of gas. The SBR would remain in use into the Second World War.

21 When going into the line the helmet replaced the cap and the respirator was moved into the middle of the wearer's chest. Worn in this position it was possible for the face piece to be put on in a few seconds whilst a corrugated rubber hose connected this to the filter in the satchel. The advantage of this was that the filter could be large, increasing endurance in the gas cloud, but the weight of the filter was taken on the wearer's shoulders not his face, unlike German masks.

22 The final item required is the rifle, the standard Short Magazine Lee Enfield (SMLE). Adopted in 1907, it would still be in use at the end of the Second World War. With a ten-round magazine and 'soldier-proof' reputation, the SMLE was one of the great rifles of both world wars.

23 Although the soldier might be loaded to his satisfaction, the NCOs would also have ideas about what might still be required. Soldiers going into the line would need to take with them additional stores, flares, rockets or rations. Sandbags were a useful and plentiful means of carrying whatever was issued to the men.

Despite his appearance the 'model' for this section is a serving soldier of the Royal Logistic Corps provided by 25th Training Regiment RLC.

23. This rear view shows the way in which the soldier's load is distributed. One cartoon of the period has a boy ask 'What is a soldier for?' The answer is 'Something to hang things on'!

THE TRENCHES IN ACTION

When considering a trench system the frontline tends to be a dominant feature in most people's imagination of the Western Front. It is here we imagine that the war was principally fought, as this is the place from which assaults are launched and upon which the enemy mounted raids or dropped shells. Unfortunately, it is also the frontline that is illustrated in most textbooks and shown in television documentaries or dramas about the war. One could be forgiven for believing that both sides had a thin line of trenches facing each other across no-man's land with little behind the frontline other than the artillery positions and training camps. In reality, for every 1 mile of frontline, there were miles of trenches behind it providing successive lines of defence, communication systems, rest areas, shelters and headquarters. Some of these were far out of sight of the frontline but were still linked to it by trenches. This zone could be several miles deep and became more elaborate as the war progressed.

If a soldier was sent to the frontline, he would probably start his journey by night in order to avoid enemy observation, several miles from his final destination. At Ypres in early 1917, this would mean marching down the road that ran alongside the railway line from Poperinge. During this journey he would pass numerous medical facilities, depots and gun lines, and the road would be busy with soldiers, horse-drawn and motor vehicles going in both directions, some heading for the city of Ypres in the heart of the Salient and the others away and to safety. Next, he would pass through the ruined city, home to thousands of soldiers living in the cellars and fortifications, and then leave through one of its eastern gateways, the most famous of which was the Menin Gate. In the Great War, this was simply a gap in the seventeenth-century ramparts with a raised roadway across the old moat. The standing joke of the period was 'Would the last person out of the Menin Gate please turn the lights off'. The next leg of the journey was fraught with danger as there was no continuous line of trenches until some distance from the city. The most dangerous areas were landmarks which were visible on the shell-torn landscape and also marked on maps by both sides. This allowed accurate shelling of these points. The road junction where the road to Menin was crossed by several other routes was aptly named 'Hell Fire Corner' by the troops. This area, despite the use of camouflage screens, was frequently shelled and the number of smashed wagons and dead horses that abounded here created the tell-tale smell of the Salient: mud and decay. From here, depending upon their final destinations, the men and horses took different routes. The animals and horse-drawn vehicles stayed on the various tracks to the gun positions, batteries and dumps, whilst the men descended into the relative safety of the first sinuous 'Communication Trenches' (CTs). Even for a man carrying just his personal kit and equipment the curving nature of these trenches increased the distance to a destination and made keeping direction difficult. The reason for these curves was to prevent enemy weapons being able to fire along a trench and to reduce the damage liable to be caused by a shell bursting in the system. However, the curves and angles in the trench could not be too tight. This was to ensure that a loaded stretcher could be carried along it. If the curves had a radius of less than 16ft (5m) a stretcher would not fit. The up-cast earth from the excavation of the trench was thrown up on both sides to provide additional protection to men using the system, but this did prevent soldiers seeing out and using conventional landmarks to provide some means of orientation. One consequence of this was the use of trench names, sometimes humorous or references to familiar places at home. On other occasions the whole system was named with a common letter so that it was possible to calculate roughly where you were with reference to a map, as the 'S' trench names related to the 'S' map square in which they were located. Despite this, it was easy to get lost and many soldiers new to an area tramped in the wrong direction for hours before being redirected by a friendly 'native'.

To ensure that it was possible both to move laterally and to provide positions to support the frontline, someone moving to the front would find lateral trenches intersecting with the CTs at various distances from the frontline. These 'Reserve Trenches' were planned so that they could give supporting fire to more advanced positions or natural features, such as likely routes of attack. These trenches would be occupied by the second line or support troops and because of their position would enjoy better conditions than the frontline. They would have a more liberal provision of dugouts, often housing headquarters, ammunition and engineers' stores and medical posts. As smoke or the glare from fires was not potentially as dangerous in these trenches as it was in positions closer to the frontline, it was also possible to make a more liberal use of braziers in cold weather and to have semi-permanent kitchens.

The next stage forward was the area of the 'Support Trenches', which were roughly 150ft (46m) behind the frontline. These trenches could provide close support to the front and were a first line of refuge in case of a successful enemy attack. To help with this some sections were designed for all-round defence as 'Strong Points'. These were intended to hold out even if an enemy attack got past the position. They also had reserve supplies of food and ammunition and, in theory, could hold out until a counterattack took place. The support trenches were better provided than the frontline with dugouts and shelters, but the troops in them would have to be prepared to defend both the most advanced line and the routes to and from it. In consequence, the ends of the communication trenches would be fitted with barbed-wire obstacles and bombing pits from which defenders could throw grenades into a captured length of trench.

The final step on the move to the front was that to the frontline itself. This area was at best spartan and could be very primitive. Due to the proximity of the enemy, this line was not well provided with anything beyond the most necessary shelters and dugouts, and the garrison would spend most of their time in a basic trench. However, even here certain defensive principles dictated the layout of the 'Frontline Trenches'. The most advanced area was termed the 'Fire Bay' and was provided with a 'Fire Step' so that the troops making up the garrison could use their weapons whilst standing. To reduce the risk of an enemy being able to fire along the length of the trench and to localise the effect of shells, each fire bay was limited to no more than 30ft (10m) with a traverse of roughly half this length between a pair of fire bays. Critically these traverses were not designed to be used as firing positions to prevent men in the rear of a fire bay shooting a comrade who appeared in front of him by mistake. In all areas, this system was adapted to take account of the local topography and ground conditions and in ideal circumstances a second line of trenches known as the 'Supervision Trench', liberally provided with shelters, existed 40ft to 60ft (12m to 18m) back from the frontline.

No frontline trench could survive without barbed wire to slow down attackers. The first entanglement was constructed not less than 60ft (20m) in front of the position with a second, if possible, the same distance again away. It was suggested that each of these be at least 30ft (10m) wide, but no more than 2ft 6in high, 'a greater height only increases its liability to be damaged by our own fire'. As most soldiers were well above 5ft tall this may have resulted in some nervous soldiers working in no-man's-land.

If the nature of the ground allowed for it, many frontline positions extended well into no-man's-land, both beneath and through the wire entanglements. Listening saps extended out from the forward trench so that the defenders could have advanced warning of the enemy's intentions or to provide fire along the line of the barbed wire in the event of an attack. In some areas, mining and counter-mining meant that in the area between the trenches were mine craters and these were prepared for defence, especially in situations where the lips of the craters were above ground level. Troops in these advanced positions were very isolated, often cut off by their own wire and with little hope of escape in the event of an enemy attack. They were, however, the most advanced eyes and ears of the defenders and their vigilance could save hundreds, if not thousands, of lives.

COOKING IN THE TRENCHES

The soldier has assembled the utensils and ingredients to make a cup of trench tea. He has used his entrenching tool to scrape out a slot in the trench wall wide enough to take the Tommy cooker and support his mess tin.

From top to bottom:

With the cooker protected by the earth on three sides and the mess tin above it is possible to heat water in even the worst weather. All that is required is a match to light the gel.

In this demonstration the tea is being added to the still boiling water. Measuring was a matter of guesswork and trench tea was famous for being both very strong and sweet.

Milk is added to the tea in the mess tin. With no tea bags or sieves, a favourite trick was to drop a headless match into the brew. This floated and, in theory, attracted the loose leaves so they could be flicked away before the tea was drunk.

Although hot rations and drinks could be sent up to the frontline trench from the rear it was vital that the men were able to at least heat water for a drink or washing even if they could not cook a full meal. Doing this quickly and with little tell-tale smoke is an art and requires no little skill. Many soldiers purchased, or had bought for them, a small Primus stove which used methylated spirits. Simpler to operate, as it used a gel rather than liquid fuel, was the so-called 'Tommy Cooker' which could be purchased in many department stores or in a canteen behind the lines.

To operate the Tommy cooker it was only necessary to remove the lid and place the tin windshield and support on top of the burner. Once the soldier's mess tin or a cup was filled with water from a water bottle the process started.

The intense and smokeless flame heated the water very quickly and in less than 3 minutes the contents of the mess tin was at a rolling boil. The water was now ready for a wash or a cup of tea. The ration issued to each man included tea, sugar and condensed milk. This soldier has a private purchase two-part tin each half of which can contain a proportion of tea and sugar. Without this, the precious leaves and granules would end up in an old cigarette tin or worse still loose in a twist of paper. Once the water was up to temperature the cooker could be extinguished by placing the lid on top of the fuel, cutting off the oxygen supply at once. The tin, however, remained hot for a long time and care had to be taken not to pop it into a haversack before it was cool. It was also important to place the used mess tin inside the issue mess tin cover to prevent soot and ash being transferred to uniform and equipment.

A soldier's ration included 3oz (85g) of sugar per day. This was a significant contribution towards the calories he expended in the trenches, especially in wet and cold conditions. Additional sugar was provided by the condensed milk that was the only variety available in the frontline. Once opened the contents of a tin would have been shared among the members of the section quickly as there was no way to reseal the pierced tin.

For a soldier who did not have access to a Tommy cooker an alternative was to improvise using materials which came easily to hand. One of the most well-known techniques involved cutting a sandbag into strips and soaking these in melted candle wax. Once this had hardened, it could be stored in a watertight tin or, as it was waterproof, simply loose in a pocket ready for use. The technique is similar to that for the Tommy cooker, although the pieces of sandbag are simply placed on the floor of the pre-made cut in the trench side.

The waxed sandbag burns quickly and with a bright flame. As with the Tommy cooker, the water heats quickly and although the tin becomes quickly sooty on its base there is virtually no smoke.

The only problem with the sandbag technique was the waste involved. As it was not possible to snuff out the fire efficiently it was necessary to let the precious material burn out or attempt to salvage what was left by putting a mess tin cover on the flames.

Although this works, just, it also results in a cloud of smoke. This would be very useful to enemy observers and even if it did not result in incoming fire, it would allow them to monitor the daily routine in the trench.

Another technique for trench cooking which was also, apparently, smokeless used pieces of dry wood. These were split into small slivers with a jackknife and kept in a dry place ready for use. The wood could be found easily in the trenches where most ammunition and grenades were supplied in boxes. Strictly these should have been returned to store for reuse but photographic evidence indicates that many provided fuel for heating and cooking.

Although the oil-soaked cloth lights easily and the wood soon catches fire there is an immediate problem even though the wood is very dry. The fire smokes and on a still day this tends to form a plume over the site of the fire. Although a well known method of heating water, it suggests that in reality this method could only be used in a quiet sector or at night when smoke would not be an issue.

It is through these improvisations and understanding the logistics of trench living that we really get close to what a day in the life of a trench Tommy was like.

1. A match applied to the frayed end of the waxed strip causes it to burst into flames at once.

2. The flames from this type of cooking fire would be a problem at night unless the location was well below the parapet.

3. With the burnt and blackened sandbag 'out', smoke continues to be given off for some time and the burning embers tend to reignite.

4. Photographed from no-man's-land, this shows the amount of smoke produced by trying to put out the sandbag cooker.

5. The base of the fire is a fragment of rifle cleaning cloth which has been used and is well soaked in oil. The other pieces are built up to create a miniature bonfire.

6. What appears to be steam is in fact smoke from the developing fire. Even when all the wood is burning there is still plenty of smoke given off.

BUILDING THE TRENCH

For the purposes of *24hr Trench*, we built a tiny section of trench system on an area of disused agricultural land in Surrey. This piece of experimental archaeology has no precedent in the United Kingdom. Although replica trench systems have been built for film or television and some for museums, the requirements of film directors and the rules governing health and safety have introduced a wide range of compromises. These would mean that a Great War soldier would have been immediately aware that he was in a fake. To avoid this happening for the replica to be used in the book we went back to the very basics of original trench construction.

The popular impression of trenches is that they were always muddy and surrounded by flooded shell holes; however, these conditions depended upon the local geology, not the nature of the war. Some sectors were dry, well drained and rarely flooded even in the worst weather. Others around Ypres where the water table was high were liable to flood. In the worst areas where water was found just below the surface, trenches were not dug down, but built up using earth from behind and in front of the command trench. However, flooding also requires rain so the time of year has an important part to play in trench conditions. The first day of the Battle of the Somme in June 1916 and that of Third Ypres, otherwise known as Passchendaele, in July 1917 were marked by hot weather.

As the intention was to recreate trench life in winter it is was unlikely that, even with global warming, it would be hot in January. What remained to be seen was what the soil was like below the turf on the chosen site. A little work using a geological auger produced the evidence we were looking for. Below the topsoil and a band of crushed brick which had once been a tennis court was clay. Not just a band of clay, but thick layers ranging in colour from light yellow to blue. As the location chosen was on the border of Surrey and West Sussex, what we had found was Wealden clay. Building the system here would be inappropriate to try to match the chalk of the Somme on the southern British sector of the Western Front. The closest match was the Ypres Salient famous for the mud and flooding. Although I had been involved in archaeological projects around Ypres and know the area well, the sites on which I had worked did not match the hillside location in Surrey. Here the site is just below the top of a low ridge that runs from north-east to south-west. This matched the conditions found in the Salient where the Germans had the advantage of holding higher ground than the British for most of the war. A quick look at a trench map provided a good match for both geology and topography. Not far from the famous Menin Road, which runs east from Ypres is the small village of Hooge. This area saw bitter fighting from 1914 to the end of the war and in addition to the first use of flamethrowers on the battlefield was an area of extensive mining by both sides. The wooded nature of the site and proximity to the hill summit indicated that we would have to match these features in the historical prototype. This led to the choice of the front face of Railway Wood where the Allied lines were opposite the German trenches across a no-man's-land broken by numerous mine craters and where the shattered stumps of trees were such a feature of the battlefield. To the north of the wood the railway from Ypres to Roulers, behind German lines, ran in cuttings that provided cover for men from both sides. The bed of the railway also offered useful materials to improve trenches and dugouts and this suggested that railway sleepers would add some authenticity to the replica. In reality, the track was used to reinforce overhead cover for many dugouts, but railway track is expensive to buy and rather difficult to cut so this feature was omitted.

A quick study of trench maps indicated that the British frontline trench ran along the edge of Railway Wood facing north-east and that various communication trenches angled back under the remaining cover of the trees. Based on the size of the site it was decided there was sufficient space to build a section of frontline with two full-size fire bays, a couple of protective traverses and a communication trench running back down the hill and allowing access to the frontline. To provide a variety of other typical features it was decided to include a dugout on one side of the communication trench and a latrine on the other.

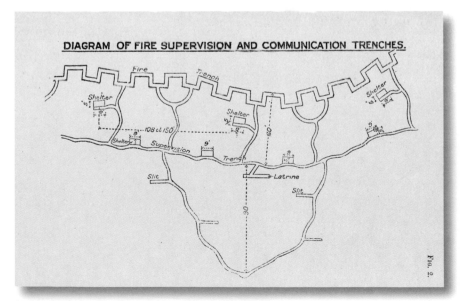

An idealised trench as shown in one of the many manuals.

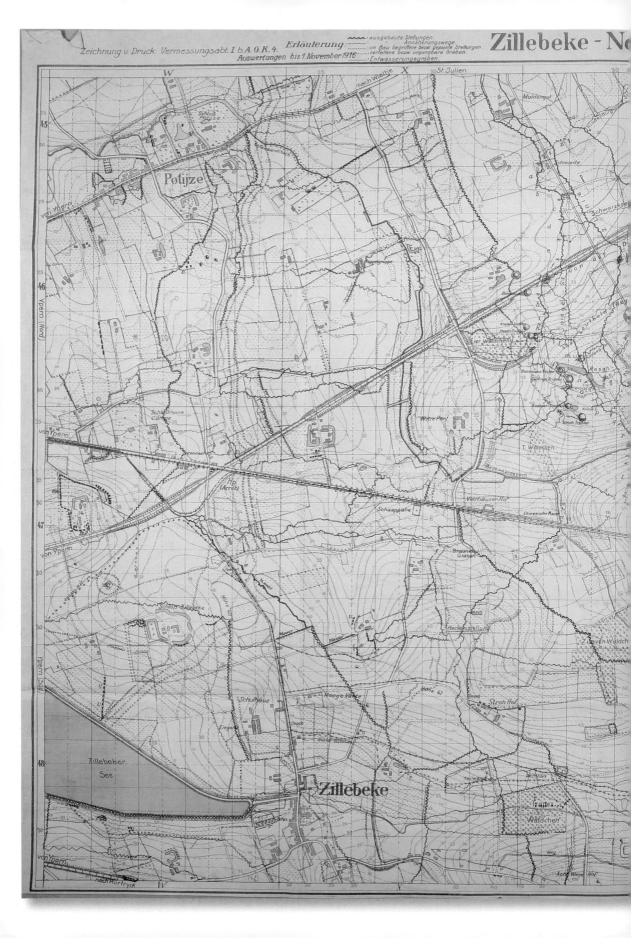

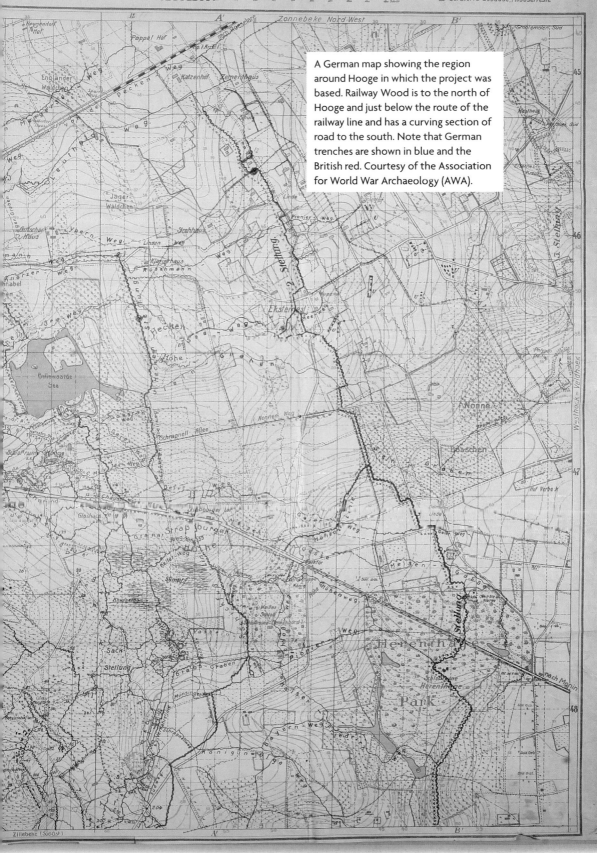

A German map showing the region around Hooge in which the project was based. Railway Wood is to the north of Hooge and just below the route of the railway line and has a curving section of road to the south. Note that German trenches are shown in blue and the British red. Courtesy of the Association for World War Archaeology (AWA).

As the dugout could only accommodate a limited number of people, an infantry shelter or 'shallow dugout' was planned for the frontline together with a 'kitchen' area. This last feature does not appear in contemporary manuals but a good example of one can be seen a piece of British film from 1917.

To ensure that the replica was as authentic as possible we used a combination of trench manuals, original photographs, memoirs and film as our sources. It was clear from the Great War archaeology some of the team had been involved in previously that real trenches do not match the training manuals. The trenches shown are idealised versions of what should be achieved. This is well illustrated by *Entrenching Made Easy*, an interesting idea in itself, and *Knowledge for War: Every Officer's Handbook for the Front*. The instructions here are clearly given for men to practise in training areas well away from the front and in daylight. In reality, trenches could only be constructed under cover of darkness, as the proximity of the enemy meant that any work carried out that was spotted by the opposing troops would attract fire. This is well demonstrated by Edmund Blunden in *Undertones of War*. In 1916, he was 'Works Officer' in the village of Auchonvillers about 1,000m, just over half a mile, from the frontline. The village could be observed from the German position and even on a quiet day, they were clearly vigilant. He and a fellow officer were working on a sump 'six feet below the trench bottom – and it would have been deeper, but in the obsession of rapture we flung up a shovelful of earth over the parapet, and the observant Germans gave us notice with several large and well-placed shells'.

Digging trenches in daylight is hard work, doing the same in semi-darkness has to be tried to be appreciated and, for the purpose of the project, virtually all of the work took advantage of daytime. As another concession, we also used machinery to speed up the initial digging in. Although using a JCB can be seen as cheating the number of men available during the Great War, when tens of thousands of soldiers inhabited each mile of line, was not replicated for the project. This does not mean that soldiers were not involved in building the replica and the first stage of construction was carried out by ten members of 23rd Pioneer Regiment of the Royal Logistic Corps. They arrived on a Monday morning in May with a mini bus and Land Rover and set up camp on site for five days of work. An array of hand and power tools was already available and vital 'trench stores' such as metal angle iron, corrugated sheets, wire and timber had been assembled. Some of this had to be purchased while a local timber mill, reclamation company and a helpful quartermaster donated the majority. A small amount of trench boards and some of the sign boards had been used on the set of the film *War Horse* and were delivered to the site with some equipment used as patterns by the film's prop department.

The covering of grass and brambles had already been cut down with a mower towed behind a tractor and this allowed the site to be marked out. Originally, this would have been done with pins and white tape as this would show up in the dark. As we were working in daylight and with a digger, we chose tents pegs and orange plastic tape so the digger operator could see where to work. It was very odd to be pacing about the site armed with a hammer, tape, pegs, a tape measure and an original manual to ensure that the size and layout was correct. In less than 4 hours, immensely quicker than had we attempted it by hand, the basic trench system was finished and a series of 'shell craters' had been created. The spoil was dumped in front or behind the trench ready to be used as sandbag fill or to create the parapet and parados. With the digger off site, it was possible to get to work with hand tools. The big discovery at this point was that although the topsoil was easy to dig only a few inches down the clay was baked hard. Below that, the clay was stiff and unyielding. It stuck to tools like glue and if left exposed for more than a few hours would start to harden like a ceramic. There was much cursing and most of the team were soon nursing aching backs and blistered hands. One constant topic of conversation between the soldiers was the comparison between their work with the assistance of mechanisation and the reality of trench digging by hand in the Great War. As virtually all of them had seen service in Iraq and Afghanistan, and had returned from operations a few months earlier, it was interesting to hear what respect they had for their predecessors. Equally striking was the amount of physical work they had been required to carry out in the modern campaign. Digging trenches and dugouts can be compared to the construction of modern Forward Operating Bases (FOBs) and defensive positions that are still needed even in modern warfare.

With the benefit of hindsight, it is clear that we should have spent far longer cutting the earth back to slope the sides of the trench left by the digger. The Great War manual makes it clear that vertical sides to a trench will collapse and that an angle of about one in four is preferable. Because we had plenty of corrugated-iron sheets and metal stakes, we all agreed that it 'would hold'.

We were proved very wrong in the months that followed. In the four remaining days the Pioneers laboured to revet the trench walls, built fire steps, roofed over a section of the communication trench and erected barbed-wire defences. Nearly 100 sheets of corrugated iron were used up and we made three round trips to the wood yard to collect an amazing assortment of timber, nails, staples, saws and chicken wire. At the end of the week, they were especially proud of a tunnel built to connect the trench with a shell hole in the newly created no-man's-land.

A line drawing of the trench system and dugout. Courtesy of Bob Moulder.

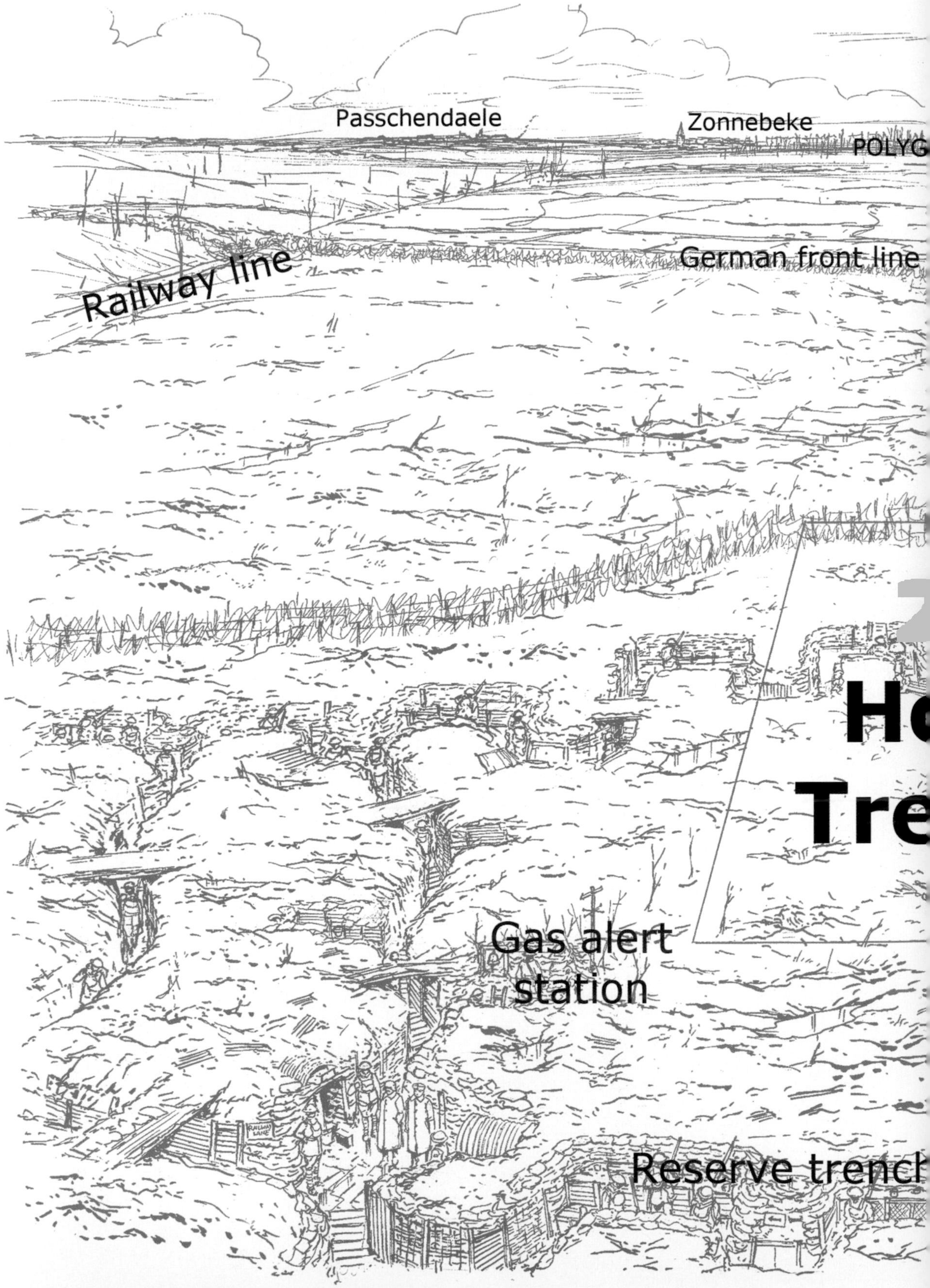

Passchendaele

Zonnebeke

POLYG

Railway line

German front line

H
Tre

Gas alert
station

Reserve trench

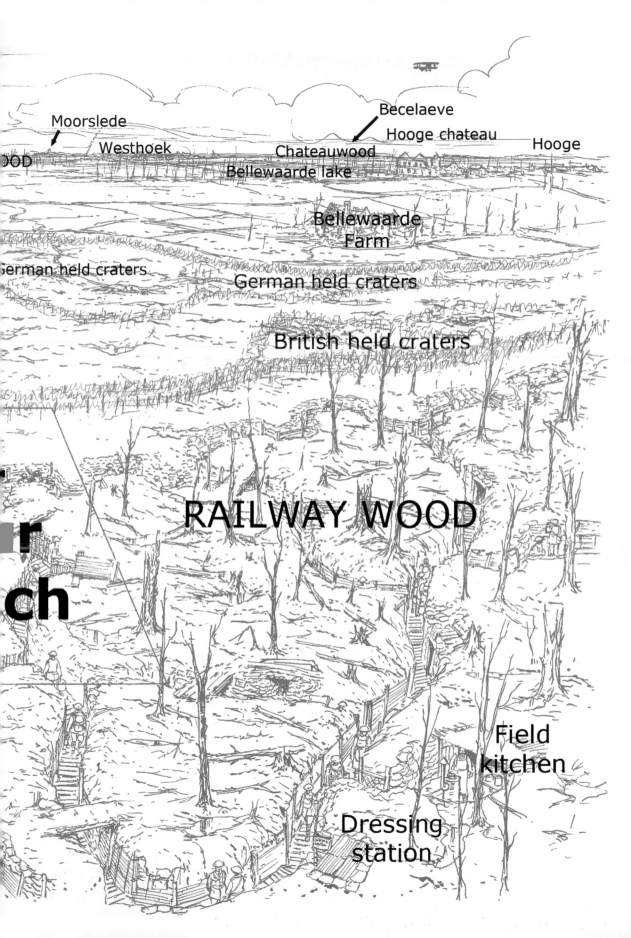

Moorslede

OOD

Westhoek

Becelaeve

Hooge chateau

Chateauwood

Hooge

Bellewaarde lake

Bellewaarde
Farm

German held craters

German held craters

British held craters

r
ch

RAILWAY WOOD

Field
kitchen

Dressing
station

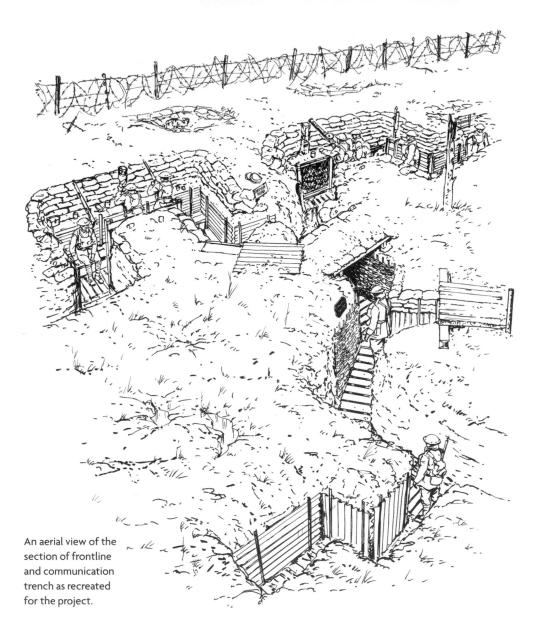

An aerial view of the section of frontline and communication trench as recreated for the project.

On the last day, while some of the group loaded the Land Rover with the tentage and beds, three of the Pioneers put on replica Great War uniforms, real equipment, helmets and other kit so they could 'try out' the trench in appropriate kit. They announced that modern kit is far superior but were amazed to discover that the pattern standard shovel of the Great War, the General Service or GS, is still in use today after virtually 100 years.

To ensure that the trench weathered and settled down, we left the system alone for most of the next few months and returned to start work in September. By that time, the site was a profusion of brambles and weeds plus quite a few flowers. These included cornflowers and poppies, the symbol of Great War and later remembrance.

Above: The interior of the dugout as planned.

Left: The infantry shelter as planned. This feature became known as the 'ice box' when used by the garrison.

Members of 23rd Pioneer Regiment RLC in the finished trench.

Although using a digger might appear to be cheating even with lots of volunteers digging trenches is incredibly time consuming and exhausting.

A section of trench which we thought would survive. Weather and gravity proved us wrong. Later playing dams in the trench kept us busy but did not improve the drainage.

For some visitors to the site this was a bit of a shock and more than a few suggested that vegetation like this was historically incorrect, as they pointed out all the photographs that they had seen showed either the interior of the trenches or the barren moonscape of no-man's-land left behind after heavy fighting. As we were aiming to portray a relatively quiet sector of the line in winter, and it would be winter when we took the photographs, I decided to leave the vegetation as it was. Much of it would be crushed under foot as we worked on the trench and the areas under the barbed wire would have been as inaccessible during the war as they were now. By the time we did the photography, the flowers had withered and we cut back anything that got in the way around the trench.

The rest was left as a reminder that nature can overwhelm the work of many even during a war. This aspect of spring and summer when flowers sprouted in the most unlikely parts of the war-torn land is frequently mentioned in memoirs by the men who served in the trenches. It is, however, surprising to the generations who grew up with black-and-white images and film-set reconstructions as a reference that I had to fight hard against a scorched-earth policy to make the replica 'more realistic'.

Once the frontline was more or less established what remained to be done was some sort of drainage and the construction of a shelter for the men in the frontline and a dugout. One of the features of excavating original trenches is the importance placed upon discovering where drains and sumps were dug. Frequently items dropped by soldiers in the trenches fall on to the trench boards to be knocked between the slats before being washed away into the drainage channel or ending up at the bottom of the sump. In the village of Auchonvillers these areas in a single section of communication trench yielded items as varied as ammunition, buttons, coins and a finger ring. We took care to copy the manual and two of us spent a happy afternoon building miniature dams and drains. I do not think it made the slightest difference to the water level, but it did produce an area in which an unsuspecting walker could step into a thigh-deep hole once the trench board was removed.

One feature of wet sectors of the trenches was the use of wooden 'A' Frames, or 'Short Revetting Frames', to both resist the pressure of the clay on both sides of the trench and to support the trench boards or 'duck boards' above the water level. Because the frames are virtually submerged in the water table, they tend not to rot away. They are found in significant numbers on archaeological sites around Ypres. I had been given one of these original frames that had been dis-covered by the Association for World War Archaeology (AWA) in the Salient. This, together with the drawing from a manual provided for the replica we built, was put into place. One feature of the use of the 'A' Frames was that the trench boards have to sit so that the end of one board can fit into the next one and so that both rest on the frame. The manual also mentioned that covering the top of the board with chicken wire improved grip for the soldiers' boots and helped make the board fireproof! We added the wire, but judging by the water level fire was the least likely problem the boards would face.

The shelter and dugout were not so easy to construct and were a perfect illus-tration of an additional range of problems that faced the men of the Great War. So far, the trench had been built using material that could be carried forward down a communication trench as separate elements. Two men could carry three or more sheets of corrugated iron and one man three 6ft-long steel stakes. A single man could carry a bundle of fifty sandbags to be filled in the frontline. Shelters and dugouts, as the manual showed, required prefabricated panels to be built off site and then put into position. This, we theorised initially, was to reduce the tell-tale construction noise and speed up the process. We later discovered that it is actually impossible to build the panels in the cramped conditions of a hole in the ground when it is dark. As I lived near the site, I was very proud of my first effort to build a side wall for the shelter. It was constructed from heavy timbers to make a frame covered with a skin of corrugated iron. It only took an hour or so to make and at the end of my time as carpenter I was curious to see how it would look in the hole previously dug by the JCB. I immediately discovered a problem. I could not lift the finished panel, let alone drop it into the hole. This simple and obvious point illustrated an entire area of trench warfare I had never appreciated. The men in the frontline did much of the building and maintenance of the trenches but anything that required skilled Engineers, Pioneers and members of the labour battalions, such as carpentry, took place behind the lines. Once finished the 'fatigue parties' would have to manhandle these unwieldy structural elements along the communication trenches to the point they were required – in the dark!

To replicate the process of wartime construction we established an outdoor workshop where, using trestles and the fast-diminishing piles of material, we built eleven frames, of different sizes, together with additional trench boards, roof sections and a couple of hurdles to reinforce weak sections of the trench wall. As each piece was finished it was manhandled to its intended location. Luckily, this did not include much transport down the trench. However, when we did this on a couple of occasions we discovered that a 6ft section only just fits along a communication trench, under overhead cover and round the corner of a traverse. We also found out that putting the section together with hammer and nails made a lot of noise even if the holes had been pre-drilled. This left the question of how anything was constructed in proximity to the enemy. If rhythmic hammering was located, bullets would follow. Not too bad if you were working below ground level on a dugout entrance, but suppose the enemy employed mortars or artillery? Perhaps, the idea of both sides 'turning a blind eye' to activity in the opposing sector in the interest of 'starting anything' also included 'turning a deaf ear'?

The biggest problem with both these structures proved not to be their construction, but the preparation of the pit into which they fitted. The JCB had done a good job in creating a hole with semi-vertical sides marginally larger than the intended panels. Unfortunately the floor was concave in both cases and the pit slightly too narrow. We thought it would be a simple task to square the pits off and throw the earth up on to the surface. This did not prove to be the case. Despite the use of pickaxes to break up the clay and the sharpest spades, we found the process took hours. To make it worse, it proved impossible to throw the excavated clay up as it stuck to the shovels and did not fit into buckets. We were forced to hand blocks of clay up to the surface or squash it into sandbags for use elsewhere on site.

The roof for the infantry shelter, as it is called in the manual, was formed from overlapping sheets of curved corrugated iron placed so that the weight of the earth thrown on top was resisted by the upward curve. Luckily for us, the manual indicated that the earth roof was to be no more than 1ft (30cm) of earth.

An example of one section of dugout wall. Impossible to move on your own and a nightmare even with a team in the dark.

This meant that the structure was concealed from observation, but that any sense of safety offered to the occupants was an illusion. The earth roof and iron sheets 'might' stop a small piece of shell fragment or shrapnel ball, but anything bigger would go straight through. Worse still, if a shell hit the top it would explode, having penetrated the earth and struck something more solid such as the roof or interior. If that happened there would have been no survivors. The dugout, as its name implies, was meant to be far deeper and therefore safer. We discounted the idea of mining, as a collapse would be fatal. This left the method used for shallow dugouts 'cut and cover'. Essentially a hole is excavated and the dugout built within this before a substantial covering is put on top. To make it historically accurate we built the roof from beams and corrugated iron. Above this, we used a layer of railway sleepers and steel 'I' beams. On top of this, we applied a final layer of earth covering. In theory, a shell striking the top or entrance of the dugout would pass through the earth before hitting the layer of steel and heavy timbers. This would detonate the shell; almost certainly stunning the dugout's occupants and blowing out the candles, but with luck not killing everyone.

Above: Even squaring off a pit dug by a JCB was backbreaking. Digging a hole for a dugout by hand must have been daunting. *Below:* The partially completed dugout showing the bunks built from chicken wire like the originals. Despite all our hard work the weather rapidly gets the upper hand. One of the horrors of trench warfare.

To make the structure more comfortable we added two bunks at one end using chicken wire as the base of the 'bed'. At the other end, we left a hole through which the chimney of a stove could project. Originally, the chimney would have been constructed from large food tins and we used the same technique.

We were immensely proud of our efforts and on the final Sunday, we had a walk round to admire the 'finished' system and take some photographs as a record. Unfortunately, we had not allowed for 'enemy activity'. This did not take the form of shelling, but was just as devastating. In the weeks before Christmas, it rained heavily and I did not visit the site. When I eventually ventured out on a dry morning between Christmas and New Year's Eve what I discovered was a shock. With the weight of the additional water added to the existing clay and sandbags whole sections had failed. One end of the trench had collapsed; the 'kitchen' had ceased to exist and could only be identified by the few cans from the chimney that now lay at the bottom of the trench. Worse still, the central traverse which lay between the two fire bays had effectively 'run' like a liquid. Sandbags that had been on the surface now lay virtually at ground level. Metal stakes had been twisted and, in one area, a frame placed at an angle to support the back wall of the trench was now vertical and useless. All of this damage was an object lesson in the problems faced by the men in the trenches. Even without enemy action whole systems were damaged by frost, rain and rot. To keep the trenches usable the garrison and hundreds of thousands of men behind the lines were busy building, repairing and improvising every day of the war. Even the most 'perfect' section of trench could be brought down by heavy rain or the effect of enemy gunfire. Although I had been aware that trenches require maintenance, I had no real idea how time- and material-consuming this task really was in practice.

One curious result of this experience was a discussion with a serving army officer. He commented on what a good thing it was for the officers of the Great War that all this work was necessary. When I challenged him on it being a 'good thing' his response was to point out that soldiers with little to do are a problem in peacetime or in a war. If they could be kept busy on useful, even life-saving tasks, such as trench construction and maintenance, they would never be bored. As it was we shared some of the original frenetic activity and in the final days before the photography a small army of helpers dug away fallen sections of trench, built new sandbag walls and generally tidied up. The kitchen never got rebuilt and the first task the 'garrison' had to face when they took over their section of the frontline was to repair the most recent weather damage. In many ways it was just like the real thing.

THE 'REAL' 24 HOURS

The decision was taken to stage the photography over a 24-hour period at the time of year that matched the original. This meant that we were going to be putting a representative group of volunteers into a replica trench system in the middle of winter and asking them to recreate virtually every aspect of day-to-day life in the Ypres Salient in January 1917. Our reference for the 24 hours was the battalion War Diary of the 1/5th Liverpool Regiment.

The diary for 1 and 2 January records the following:

1st January: Weather fine. Observation good. Much aerial activity. Hostile artillery action for ¾ of an hour about 6pm in reply to our own artillery bombardment of enemy trenches L [left] of Railway Wood.
5 of our men killed by shell in dugout in BEEK TRENCH. Casualties 5 killed, 4 sick.

2nd January: particularly quiet on our front – Relieved by 6th Battalion The Kings. Relief complete at 7.15pm. Btn [Battalion] proceeded to usual reserve dugouts in YPRES.
Causalities [sic] nil.

Support tent in place. Ready for the arrival of the 'garrison'.

An overview of a fire bay showing how the ground has slumped under the effects of rain and gravity.

Members of the section sew on insignia prior to 'going into the line'.

Above: The section poses for a team photograph, typical of the Great War before their turn in the line.
Below: The section and support team 24 hours later.

The section corporal helps to adjust the platoon sergeant's haversack. It is easy to see how much is being carried.

Having largely completed the trenches we put up a military tent close to the location to provide changing facilities and cover for the support staff on the Friday before the chosen weekend.

It was already clear that although we had organised rations, equipment, stores, tools and some pyrotechnics we were going to struggle with the condition of the trenches. One of the team pointed out that certain areas matched the aftermath of the German bombardment of 1 January 1917.

Despite gallant efforts by the support team to get everything shipshape, it was very apparent that the first job the garrison would have to do was to clear their own route into the trench system. In reality they would have taken over at night from the outgoing battalion and may well have come across similar problems. We were able to have the luxury of getting ready on a Saturday lunchtime to take over the system mid-afternoon.

Everybody who was going to be in uniform was issued with full kit if they had not provided it themselves. This meant everything from underwear to respirators and rations to handkerchiefs. It took a considerable amount of time to get the dozen men ready and there was much rearranging of packs, and distribution of tools and sandbags before they could move off to the trench.

The 'garrison' for the trench consisted of a section of ten men with a corporal and lance corporal, a platoon commander and platoon sergeant. We had a few other people available to act as runners and a medical officer and orderly. This small number of men was backed up by about half a dozen people in modern clothes including a cook, and first aiders, just in case.

To ensure that everybody knew what they were doing they had all received a copy of the 'Trench Routine' document from 1916 and the platoon commander a copy of a pamphlet from July 1916 entitled 'Some of the Many Questions a Platoon Commander Should Ask Himself on Taking Over a Trench, and at Frequent Intervals Afterwards'. He particularly liked the idea suggested on the back page which questioned whether he was as 'offensive as I might be?' The importance of this little document was to indicate the twenty-four points he was expected to observe at all times when in the trenches.

Questions ranging from the mundane such as:

14. Are the trenches as clean and as sanitary as they might be? Are live rounds and cases properly collected? Are my bags for refuse and empties in position?
15. Are your trenches as dry as I might make them?

To the critical:

16. Am I doing all I can to prevent my men from getting 'Trench Feet'?
17. How can I prevent my parapets and dugouts from falling in?

Right up to the apparently unimportant:

22. Are my men using wood from the defences as fire wood?

As the platoon commander discovered, all of these were to be problems in the next 24 hours. Even before the project started both the platoon commander and his sergeant said they were daunted by the scale of tasks that had to be tackled even without the presence of an enemy. Simply keeping the section healthy, dry, comfortable and safe was going to be difficult even if the weather was perfect. Luckily for the project the weather in 2012 was not as cold as in 1917 and the rain held off for the entire duration of the 24-hour experiment.

24HR TRENCH

07:00

It is just before dawn on the morning of Monday 1 January 1917. To the north of Railway Wood on the edge of the Ypres Salient the members of No.3 Section, 15 Platoon 1/5th King's Liverpool Regiment 'stand to' in their trench. They have been in the frontline since 28 December and in that time the weather has changed from frosty to very wet. During the previous four days, four men have been wounded and seven have reported sick. The daily routine means that at this time every morning, every man in the frontline is fully awake and armed. The men have their bayonets fixed and are standing in the trench in case of German attack. Everyone involved in trench warfare knows that dawn and dusk are the times of day when a raid or full-scale assault is most likely to occur. For men in the frontline this is part of a carefully organised daily military routine, which dictates what they do for almost every minute of the day.

Since the previous evening, one man in three has been on guard duty, 'sentry go', for 1 hour at a time, standing on the fire step with head and shoulders above the parapet. During this time they are forbidden to wear anything that might cover their ears as a sentry needs to be able to hear movement on no-man's-land even if he cannot see. With the temperature below zero and with a stiff wind blowing the men are soon freezing. Unable to duck into the relative shelter of the trench they stamp their feet and clap their hands together to keep the circulation going. Gloves, mufflers, leather jerkins and greatcoats all help, but cannot prevent the numbing effects of the cold. In early January, the moon is virtually full and the cold light illuminates the trench, its occupants and the ground in front. Clouds passing in front of the moon create the illusion of movement and men who stare at thickets of barbed wire or tree stumps can be convinced that something has moved. In these circumstances, not summoning the NCO or challenging the movement can end in death. A raiding party can slip through the wire and fall on the garrison in seconds unless a timely warning is given by the sentries. To make the situation even more serious, the men all know that falling asleep on duty or being inattentive is a military crime. A man who is discovered to have done so can be court-martialled and if found guilty executed by firing squad (although this only happened twice in practice it remained a theoretical possibility). Some men prefer to stand with their chin resting on the fixed bayonet as a means of staying awake. A few chat to comrades close to them in the

A sentry stands on the fire step staring into no-man's-land alert for any signs of an enemy attack. He is forbidden from wearing anything covering his ears so for the last hour he has been cold and tense.

The corporal batters a clay-filled sandbag into shape as the section tries to improve the trench.

A man already weary after a long night grips his rifle ready for his turn on 'sentry go'. The men know that sleeping on duty is punishable by death.

darkness discussing everything from football results to county class cricket or the prospect of a good angling season ahead. All wish away the minutes until a new sentry 'relieves' them.

Every hour another man who has been 'resting', a virtual impossibility, takes over and the outgoing man is set to work on some of the multitude of night-time tasks required to maintain the trenches. These tasks are not resented. Not only does digging or sandbag filling keep the men active, and a little warmer, the new construction may offer protection in a bombardment or help to combat the ever-rising water. In these circumstances, although the German soldiers on the other side of no-man's-land are a constant threat the real enemy is the weather, the mud and the water level.

07:30

'Stand to' is a test of training and timing. Well before twilight, all the men stand on the fire step and wait for orders. As the sun gradually rises, the darkness gives way to the first glimmers of dawn and it is possible to see more detail. On most of the Western Front the Allied lines faced virtually due east and the sun rose behind the German lines. This brought a real threat to Allied soldiers. Virtually every morning, unless it was foggy or the weather was really poor, they found themselves staring into the sun. German snipers could use this to their advantage and a moment's inattention would invite death. To make matters more serious it was not possible to use periscopes, which was the safest way to look at the enemy lines, until it was virtually full daylight. In consequence, orders were given over the entire period of 'stand to'. These allowed the men to sink gradually down from fully standing, to a stoop with head above the parapet, to a crouch with head below its cover. Eventually every man was fully concealed, his rifle and bayonet below the sandbags so it could not be seen, as this allowed the enemy to calculate the number of men in the trench. At this point sentries, one man in ten, were posted at the periscopes or lookouts with orders to report any move-ment. Only when it was fully light and the risk of attack had receded were the remainder of the men 'stood down'.

With bayonet fixed a member of the section awaits the order to step down from the parapet before daylight reveals him to the enemy.

The rum is measured using an empty OXO tin to ensure that everyone gets a fair ration.

08:15

Being stood down marks the beginning of the daytime routine; the only advantage of winter is that there are fewer daylight hours than summer. Once the men have stepped below the parapet, their world is limited to the earth walls on both sides and the view of the sky above them. For the remaining hours of daylight, they are confined to the trench constantly aware that snipers wait for the over confident or less vigilant. Tall men move about the trench system hunched to reduce their chance of being spotted and most have their helmet tilted at what they considered a 'lucky' angle. They are aware that a helmet will not stop a bullet, but that it can deflect a shrapnel ball or small piece of shell splinter. Although 'a miss is as good as a mile', anything that offers protection is worth trying.

If the men are tired after their night of labour and constant vigilance, they are about to receive their daily reward. Every morning, in most divisions, the troops receive a rum ration carefully measured out by a senior NCO. The large ceramic jar, marked Service Ration Depot (SRD) is normally carried in a protective box and stored in a dugout where it can be supervised by an officer. There was a rumour in the army that SRD actually stood for 'Seldom Reaches Destination' or 'Service Rum Dilute'. This title was very misleading and, although the theft of SRD jars was not unknown, unfortunately for those having stolen one the contents could turn out to be lime juice or other ration items which were not quite so popular as rum.

After a period on guard duty, or working in a wet, cold trench, the dark liquid is precious to chilled soldiers. To ensure that the issue is fair and every man receives the same ration the NCO uses a small Oxo tin as a measure. To avoid sharing or hoarding the fiery liquid has to be drunk under supervision, although a few 'tea-totallers' are exempt from alcohol. In some units, where the commanding officer does not approve of rum, the men receive pea soup instead. What the men think of this alternative can be imagined. Most men drink their ration in a single draft and many claim that they can feel it spread from throat to stomach and then on to their limbs. The effect is warming, and for most, only mildly intoxicating. Sadly for the heavy drinkers, the amount issued is insufficient to make a man drunk.

With one man in ten on guard duty, the remainder now turn to the next task of the day – breakfast. As the garrison of the trench has spent the night alternating between spells of guard duty and labouring they cannot send men to collect rations and stores. Instead under cover of darkness 'carrying parties' made up of men who are out of the line have been sent forward with rations, stores and equipment.

Notes for Headquarters of Battalions and Company Commanders on Trench Routine: 41st Division (February 1916) states:

> Rations and Carrying Parties – Parties should never be sent back from the firing line for supplies or water. All supplies and stores must brought up by men detailed from the reserve company. Ration and carrying parties must carry rifles and wear bandoliers (equipment not necessary). (p. 8)

These soldiers have previously been 'in the line' and are now 'resting' before returning to the trenches. Sadly 'resting' is somewhat misleading as time spent out of the line is when the men are trained, drilled and inspected. Days are spent improving skills on the firing range, learning new tactics and competing in team games, especially football. At night, a percentage of these men form the fatigue parties required to keep the frontline supplied. In the Ypres Salient, this will mean leaving the town burdened down with everything from rations to ammunition, sheets of corrugated iron or barbed wire. Everything that cannot be sent forward by wagon or pack horse has to be carried by soldiers. These stores are always heavy, often unwieldy and sometimes dangerous. Both sides know that their opponents will be engaged in this vital task and that a few shells or mortar bombs fired blindly at known routes will very likely catch men on their way into the line or on the return journey. A consequence of this is that the men have to avoid moving in the open even though this may be a quick and easy route. Instead they proceed up to the frontline using the communication trenches where obstacles including loose trench boards, loops of signal wire or returning parties of men coming the other way are a constant hazard. Despite the name boards to indicate locations in the featureless landscape it is easy to get lost.

The men claim that they can feel the rum going down into their toes and it is useful tonic after a long, cold night.

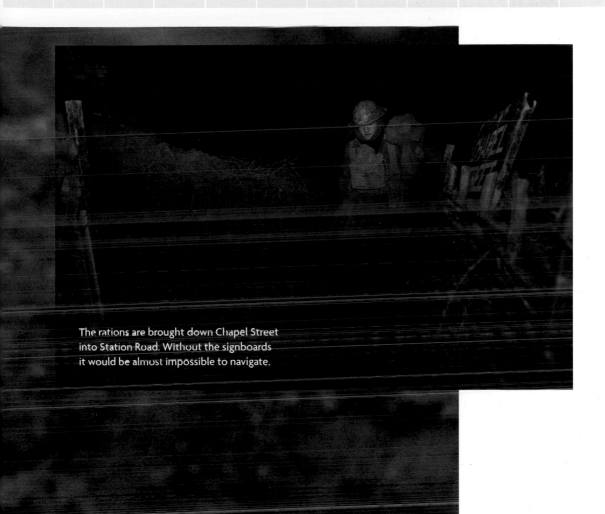

The rations are brought down Chapel Street
into Station Road. Without the signboards
it would be almost impossible to navigate.

08:30

The next part of the day is familiar, breakfast. The rations for the section arrive in a sandbag during the night and the corporal puts this in a dry corner where he can keep an eye on the contents. It is not unknown for ration items to go missing and it is always assumed that the Army Service Corps keep the best for themselves. This does not prevent the men from 'scrounging' from other platoons, but to steal from the men in one's own section would be regarded as a crime against comrades. It is important that the rations are distributed both equally and fairly.

The first task for the NCO supervising the section's rations is to see what has been delivered. Although there is a set scale of rations no two days' delivery is ever the same and there are always a few surprises and disappointments.

The rations consist of ¾lb of preserved meat, corned beef or tinned stew, more than a pound of bread or half that in biscuits, plus tea, sugar, milk, pickles and condiments. Most arrives in tins, although some items such as tea, sugar bacon or cheese are sent loose, either in paper bags or tied in the corners of a sandbag. Some of the items are easy to divide up between the men. Each soldier receives a tin of corned beef and a 'part share' of a tin of Meat and Vegetable (M&V) Stew. Tins of condensed milk are shared the same way and cheese is cut into blocks. Bread can be easily divided up, although storage in wet weather is always an issue. Jam or syrup might well arrive in a lidded tin which can be closed for future use.

The morning's share of bacon is more of a challenge. The slices of bacon purchased from a modern supermarket are a long way in the future and bacon arrives in the trench as a slab of meat ready to be cut up. This is no easy matter and it takes the combined efforts of two men, a jackknife and a very sharp bayonet to produce some rashers.

With the rations distributed there now is the question of cooking. An open fire has been burning in the corner of the trench for most of the night and the section clearly feel that the small amount of smoke being given off will not be a problem. In some sectors both sides chose to ignore activities such as this so they too could get on with breakfast. Cooking bacon in a mess tin is very tricky. The tins are made of tinned steel and if they are heated too quickly the food simply sticks to the plating and this may melt into droplets of molten metal.

Alternatives for frying include the head of a 'clean' shovel or an entrenching tool.

With all the elements for a bacon sandwich coming on it is time to 'slice' the bread. Hot water is being prepared elsewhere in the trench and tea will soon be 'on the go'. Other elements of the breakfast will be cheese and jam.

Breakfast does not have to be hurried. With the possibility of attack fading, the rest of the morning is set aside in the manual of trench routine for little more than domestic duties. This appears very relaxed, but with full daylight there is little opportunity to work on the trenches and the men are given time to recover from the long night of duties and fatigues.

The tinned items are laid out on the elbow rest in the trench so that the corporal can work out what each man should receive.

Clockwise from top left:

Bread was baked on an industrial quantity and its arrival, rather than biscuit, was always popular.

A sandbag makes a useful bread board and the elbow rest stands in for a 'breakfast bar'.

All along the British frontline men take it in turn to keep a wary eye on no-man's-land through periscopes or observation slits whilst others eat. This fire bay has no sentry so the men rely on the next bay along for a warning.

Although an unorthodox use for an entrenching tool head, the thick metal heats up well and there is no tin to melt.

Although the bayonet was a weapon it could be used as a toasting fork, tin opener or, as here, a bacon slicer.

Holding the skin taught to ensure that the razor blade does not snag is critical. Any mistake is painful and bloody. Safety razors were not issued by the army until the 1930s.

09:00

With breakfast completed the men tidy away the majority of the rations and utensils. Everyone is aware that most of this will be required for dinner (lunch) in a few hours so this is a rather hasty effort. The men hope that they will pass a rapid inspection and will not have to tidy up completely. The next stage in the day is washing and shaving. Despite the cold and mud, every man is expected to wash and shave every morning. On a freezing day, this is a test of discipline, but dirty men get diseases and unless they are clean shaved, their respirators will not seal to their faces. If this occurs, the gas will be able to get access to their eyes and mouth, the consequence of which would be all too obvious and reinforced by graphic lectures given by the unit gas officer.

With some assistance the contents of the sergeant's haversack are retrieved. What he is looking for is his 'holdall', which contains soap, 'cut throat' razor, toothbrush and powder, a comb and a towel.

Shaving requires warm if not hot water and the next task is to obtain some. Some soldiers retained a little hot water from their brew, others use cold water and a few are prepared to use the dregs of their tea as washing water. Most men manage to wash their hands and faces although a few go as far as to wash their arm pits and in summer the 'toilet' may result in a soldier standing in his underwear in a trench.

With shaving foam as yet unheard of soldiers shave using a shaving brush, water and a shaving stick. The shaving brush is used to make a lather in the lid of the mess tin and this is transferred to the face. Mirrors, usually steel, are available but most men don't use them and rely on memory to get the shaving foam in the correct places.

Shaving with the issue 'cut throat' razor is an art and serious cuts are always possible. Cold water and the lack of a mirror means that a shaver has to concentrate to avoid accidents. As each stroke of the razor removes beard it is wiped on to the towel and within a few minutes a clean-shaven soldier emerges. It is important for the NCOs to set an example to the men and everyone will shave if they have to. However, men are encouraged to grow a moustache, if they can, as this is regarded by the army as looking martial. This was enforced by military law until 1917.

09:30

With the section clean and shaved, and with all personal kit put away, it is time for the next task of the day – recycling. By 1917 every British unit had a 'salvage officer' responsible for the recovery of any equipment, kits, weapons or ration items that could be reused. Every morning the men were responsible for collecting empty tin cans, ammunition cases and dropped chargers and bullets. The unfired ammunition could be cleaned and reissued whilst empty cases and cans went to be melted down. Behind the line cooks had to hand in rabbit skins so these could be turned into gloves for airmen, and gunners were expected to return fired shell cases to be re-filled. This emphasis on recycling appears almost modern but in a world war every resource is precious and there can be no waste.

Clockwise from above:

In this case the sergeant has the luxury of using 'fresh' water heated on a methylated spirit burner. Adding water to a used mess tin also gets rid of food debris ready for the next meal, although the result can be a bit soapy.

Although stripping down to shirt sleeves for a morning wash would be convenient there are few places to put clothing and equipment in the trench. As a result a towel is used to protect kit against soap and water.

The standing orders state that every battalion will have a 'Salvage Dump' and that it is the responsibility of all ranks to salvage government property, in this case, fired rifle cases.

The Short Magazine Lee Enfield rifle has a trap in the brass butt plate inside which is stored a pull-through and brass oil bottle. This trap has to be opened and the two elements recovered as the first step in cleaning.

Men sit on the fire step as they work on their weapons, sharing oil, and cleaning cloths and tips as they work.

10:00

With the men clean, the trench tidy and everyone fed, the next part of trench routine is critically important – weapons cleaning. Despite the use of covers on the working parts, daily cleaning and the vigilance of the men, the rifles and other weapons are already starting to get muddy from the trench. Dirty weapons don't work and every rifle, pistol and machine gun has to be cleaned. As with every aspect of routine some men must remain on 'sentry go' ready to deal with any sudden attack whilst the others strip and clean their weapons. The men were taught to look after their weapon as if it was 'their wife'. Throughout their time in the trench this will never be out of reach and will require constant care if it is to work when required.

With all the rounds taken out from the magazine, an elementary safety pre-caution, cleaning can begin. Once the cleaning kit is available a piece of oiled fabric known as a '4 by 2' (from its dimensions) can be put in the loop in the pull-through and the weighted end of the cord dropped down the barrel. Once the weight appears at the muzzle it is possible to work the pull-through back and forward down the length of the barrel to remove any fouling and leave a thin coating of oil.

With the bore of the weapon cleaned it is important to pay attention to the working parts. This is the bolt that allows the weapon to be loaded. Grit here will cause wear and may prevent the rifle from working. More oil and '4 by 2' are used to remove dirt and ensure the smooth working of the parts. Too much oil, which will cause dust to stick to the metal, is regarded as being almost as bad as too little. The weapon has to be held in the air to avoid getting more dirt into any of its parts. The biggest danger is a plug of mud in the muzzle which can be caused by a moment's inattention. If fired with this in place it is almost certain that the weapon will split, rendering it inoperative and possibly injuring the firer.

The final part of the cleaning process is to ensure that the sights and other exposed metalwork are both clean and oiled. In the trenches sights are set at 200yds (182m) at all times to ensure that the firer can hit targets in no-man's-land. Having cleaned the weapons the men know that they will have to pass inspection before the dust and dirt covers can be replaced. These will also be removed during a sentry duty which will lead to another bout of cleaning to follow.

Even the platoon commander has to clean his personal weapon and by the light of a candle he works on his .455 calibre Webley revolver. With the six bullets removed, he can use a cleaning rod, oil and fabric patches to check the cylinder and barrel for signs of rust.

Dugouts are wet even with a stove burning and the combination of damp and temperature changes means that anything metal can rapidly turn red with rust.

Although not a personal weapon, grenades need to be checked on a regular basis; they are normally kept near the frontline and under cover but a few are always fused and ready in a store in the trench wall.

Grenades are not sent to the trenches with the fuse in place and a trained 'bomber', in this case the platoon sergeant, will have to insert the fuse and replace the 'live bombs' into the crate. This is not done in a crowded trench and the 'bomber' works alone so that in the event of an accident the number of casualties is reduced.

To ensure that the 'bombs' will function the base is sealed with a little Vaseline and the split pin is checked so that it can be removed when needed but will not fall out by accident. Despite the ever-present danger of enemy action, a surprisingly large number of men were killed in training accidents or in situations where weapons malfunctioned. Very often the families would be told that their loved one had died 'in action' and comrades would help to hide the painful truth.

10:30

Once a weapon has finished being cleaned it needs to be inspected to ensure that the work has been carried out satisfactorily. The platoon sergeant is responsible for all discipline questions and weapons care is a critical task. The working parts of the weapon are examined first and then, with the bolt pulled back, the bore is checked to ensure that all is in working order. A dirty rifle is a military crime and can be punished with anything from loss of pay to, in a serious repeat case, a court martial.

When cleaning the bore of the rifle it is important to keep the process even to prevent groves being formed in the barrel which will affect accuracy.

Left and above: The supply of oil is limited and this has to be carefully rationed by each soldier.

Below: An officer's pistol is privately owned but receives the same level of care as an issue weapon. In the event of his death the pistol would be returned to the family.

With the canvas curtain pulled back one of the section removes one of two crates of grenades (known as 'bombs' at the time) ready to be inspected.

Each 'bomb' is taken out of the crate in turn and with the base plug removed the 'firing set' is inserted.

Each bomb is carefully inspected and tested before being returned to the crate.

With the weapon unloaded the sergeant squints down the open barrel to check for dust, grit or over much oil. Once the weapon has been inspected it can be reloaded with ten rounds and the first round is chambered. With the safety catch applied the rifle is now ready for use.

11:00

With the morning's tasks completed some of the men are able to relax. Every man is supposed to have a rest before he does his 2 hours of daytime sentry duty. During this period he can have some time to himself, although he cannot wander about the trenches and must stay within reach of his rifle. Men received cigarettes from home and were able to buy them from canteens behind the line. One of the superstitions of soldiers was the belief that it was dangerous to light three cigarettes from the same match. The theory was that the first two would not give an enemy sniper time to take aim, but that the final one would!

Even though some men are resting a percentage of officers and men are always on duty. There are the sentries, but also one officer and another NCO who are ready to deal with any problem. The morning watch for them is from 08:30 to 12:15 and after the handover the afternoon watch is from 12:30 to 17:30.

Having completed his inspection the platoon sergeant reports to his officer in the relative safety of the dugout in the communication trench.

The Great War was run by timetable and the routine of trench warfare, shelling and attacks required accurate time keeping. Because watches of the period could lose or gain time it was necessary to 'synchronise watches'. At a predetermined time a phone call from 'higher command' would confirm the exact time and the officers and men would adjust their watches to suit.

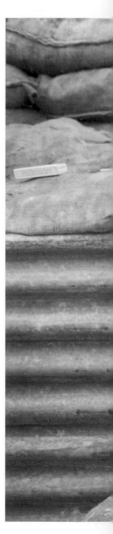

An off-duty soldier indulges in one of the few luxuries available in the trenches — smoking.
Virtually all soldiers smoked to help hide smells, ward off insects and for simple comfort in a
familiar activity.

From the entrance it is possible to look down the wood-panelled steps to the dugout below. There is no door as access is required at all times other than in the case of a gas attack.

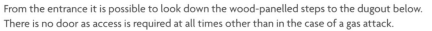

Note that the officer has a new and fashionable wristwatch which can be easily seen below his cuff whilst the NCO uses an army issue watch which is normally stored in a pocket.

11:30

In the left-hand fire bay two sentries have just changed over and the incoming man is talking to his comrade. So far it has been a quiet morning with little to report. The sentry has adjusted the periscope at a comfortable height and the top section is well wrapped in a sandbag to make it less obvious against the parapet.

While the sentries chat they are unaware that the periscope has been spotted and is being watched from within no-man's-land. Less than 100yds away a German soldier has been watching the position since dawn. Armed with a powerful telescopic sight he has watched as the periscope moved when the sentries changed over, and he has seen the tell-tale reflection of a head passing in front of the bottom mirror. He knows that the periscope is in use and that the next time the top mirror goes black a British soldier's head is just below the parapet.

As the British sentry brings his eyes back to look through the periscope a single shot hits the top mirror. The bullet cracks overhead to fly down the hill behind the position. The periscope is thrown clear from its position falling back on to the soldier's helmet with a shower of glass fragments and shattered wood. The soldiers in the bay drop down to get cover and they all look at each other to see who has been hit. Amazingly no one has been even cut by the fragments but the trench is now blind. With no way to look into no-man's-land there is every chance that a vigilant enemy will exploit the position.

With the position unable to see what is happening it is imperative that the platoon commander is told of the situation and another means of looking over the parapet quickly found. One of the section runs to the junction of the fire trench with the communication trench to summon the sergeant in the dugout.

Within a few seconds the duty officer and NCO are on the scene. Although the periscope is smashed the officer has a private purchase trench mirror called 'The Vigilant'. This will fit on to a stick or bayonet and is a good temporary replacement for the periscope. Whilst the other members of the section find the carrying bag for the periscope in which spare mirrors are stored 'The Vigilant' is put to use on the end of a bayonet.

Although this kind of activity is common, a German soldier shooting out a periscope may indicate that the enemy is becoming more offensive. A platoon commander will not be in a position to tell whether this is the case but the occurrence must be reported back to Company Headquarters and from there higher up the chain of command. With the relatively straightforward communications of the Great War this is easily done and the lieutenant returns to the dugout to telephone the captain at Company HQ.

The response from higher command is to send a sniper to find out as much as possible about the circumstances of the incident and to see if countermeasures can be employed. The first task is for the platoon commander to draw a sketch map of his position and to indicate where he believes that the shot was fired from. With no-man's-land made up of a mass of craters there are plenty of potential locations.

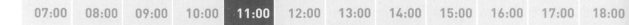

The four men in the fire bay have their rifles to hand and whilst one watches the other rest and chat waiting for their 2 hours of 'sentry go'.

The German soldier is on the edge of an old mine crater and he has built a well-camouflaged position from which to watch and wait.

Above: With the German bullet having smashed the top mirror in the periscope it is thrown clear of the parapet despite the spike and tent pegs holding it in place.

Below: Ducking under the signal wire a private is able to call for assistance without leaving his position.

Above: Whilst the sentry repairs the shattered periscope the officer positions himself so he can see over the parapet. To do so he has his back to no-man's-land but now the men in the fire bay know what is happening.
Below: The standard British field telephone of the Great War was the D3 which required a pair of cables and could be used for both Morse code and voice communication. Here the telephone is used with the voice option, although the trench location is given in code in case the enemy are listening.

The sniper with his specialist rifle and spotting scope reports to the officer and they discuss what can be done to counter the threat of enemy snipers.

12:00

It is now noon and officially time for lunch. Stew which has been prepared in the reserve line has been sent up in dixies and the men add whatever they can from their carefully hidden reserves. The stew is hot and eaten with the remains of the bread from breakfast. A few men open additional tins of Meat and Vegetable (M&V) Stew.

The best NCOs always took care to ensure that their men were looked after if not pampered. Soldiers who are hungry, cold and tired rapidly become demoralised and much more difficult to manage.

At the junction of Station Road with Chapel Street the platoon sergeant ensures that everyone gets a hot drink.

The stew is best eaten quickly as it will rapidly become a solid lump if allowed to go cold.

12:30

While dinner is being eaten the post corporal delivers the mail. Surprising though it may seem, mail was delivered from home virtually every day and even when the men were in the frontline trenches it would arrive at some point. To comply with the Defence of the Realm Act (DORA), mail was addressed by name, number and rank, a soldier's unit and British Expeditionary Force (BEF) France.

It was permissible to send all sorts of luxuries to soldiers. In addition to letters and cards, soldiers would receive food, knitwear and keepsakes from home. Contact with home was very important as it reminded the men that they had not been forgotten and souvenirs were often posted back from the trenches.

Chocolate was always very acceptable and this lucky soldier has received two bars. Shared amongst the section it will not last very long but he will expect a share from his comrades when they are more fortunate.

Men of the section share a letter from home. Very often men who were not fortunate enough to receive a letter would share the information or contents with comrades.

The platoon commander finds time to read the *Illustrated London News*, a popular periodical of the period; it allows him to keep up with current events other than the war.

13:00

The period from the end of lunch to the next 'stand to' is set aside for rest and the men, not on duty, alternate between catching a little sleep and replying to letters they have received. Sleeping in the afternoon may seem unusual but it is the warmest time of the day, even in winter, and is the least likely time for a major attack.

Although junior officers are possibly the busiest of any of the men in the trenches as they have to give orders to men under their command and take orders from above, they do get rest like everybody else. Without this they could not function and a tired officer would make mistakes which could be fatal.

By 1917 it was common to provide shelter for as many soldiers as possible even in the frontline. These may not be the deep dugouts used by headquarters but could be simple infantry shelters which would do no more than stop shell splinters but would provide cover against the elements. These were normally constructed at the rear of the trenches and fitted with blanket gas curtains in case of attack.

Soldiers were able to buy paper and envelopes from canteens, especially those run by the YMCA or from their unit. What to put into a letter was always a matter of consideration because mail was censored and the soldiers did not want to give away information that would worry their families. One familiar line was 'I hope this finds you as it leaves me, in the pink'. However, quite a few soldiers came up with code systems by which they could tell their family where they were and what they were really doing. In one case this involved putting a pin through each letter in the message to spell out the hidden information when it was held up to the light.

13:30

Taking advantage of the lull, the sniper finds a position from which he can observe the potential firing positions used by the German in no-man's-land. His intention is not to fire at this point but simply to work out where his opponent may be concealed. By this stage in the war it was often felt the best way to deal with an enemy sniper was to use an artillery barrage or mortars as there was far less risk to the men in the frontline trenches.

One of the main functions of snipers was not shooting the enemy but simply observing and reporting. This allowed the defenders to build up a picture of enemy activity, which areas of their trench were well defended, weak spots and areas which would present a good target to artillery.

Huddled in a corner an off-duty soldier gets some sleep while seated on an ammunition box. He is far from comfortable but so tired that anywhere will do.

Left: An off-duty soldier is able to remove his helmet briefly as he crouches in the doorway of an infantry shelter. Note the empty shell case used as a gas rattle to his left and the rolled up gas curtain above his head.

Above: Deep in thought, this young soldier ponders his next words in his letter home.

Above right: Viewed from the trench the sniper does not appear very well concealed, although his choice of sandbags and a good covering of mud means that he blends in well with the background.

14:00

Although using a latrine at night might be more appealing, trying to avoid the mud and accidents led to most soldiers dealing with the 'call of nature' in daylight. Permission has to be sought for a man to leave the frontline and his rifle and equipment must go with him. The latrine is in a bay off the communication trench and it is commonly believed that the size and shape of latrine pits is very similar to those used for trench mortars. This is not a place to linger. Despite that, this may be the only occasion in the day in which a soldier will be solitary. Toilet paper was not issued and soldiers improvised with whatever was available. More than a few families were surprised when a loved one requested a Bible without realising that it was not religion that motivated the request.

A soldier gives a letter from home a final reading before it is consigned to a watery grave.

The regimental medical officer (MO) and his medical orderly
approach the frontline down the communication trench.
They have with them the tools of their trade, a dry blanket
and medical outfit.

14:30

Every battalion has a single regimental medical officer, the 'MO', who with a small team of Royal Army Medical Corps (RAMC) personnel are responsible for the health of all the men in the unit. The sick are meant to report to the Regimental Aid Post (RAP) at dawn but the 'Doc' still does his 'rounds' like a doctor at home. He is especially concerned about preventable conditions related to hygiene and sanitation. This may include checking that the mess tins are clean and the soldiers' fingernails are not dirty. Early in the war 'trench foot' had been a major problem because the circulation died off in men who stood in waterlogged trenches. By 1917 this has become a matter of discipline and every soldier is expected to wear one pair of socks and have two dry pairs ready for use. To ensure that this is being done there are random inspections even in the frontline trenches.

In theory the men are supposed to remove their footwear, change their socks on a regular basis, to keep their puttees loose and in an emergency to seek help from a comrade to provide some warmth to chilled feet. This may include putting bare feet into a comrade's armpits or under his tunic. A bad case of trench foot can result in the loss of toes and the disabling of the soldier. This was regarded as preventable and trench foot became seen as a military crime rather than an ailment. The *Notes for Headquarters of Battalions and Company Commanders on Trench Routine: 41st Division* (February 1916) states that:

> It should be a point of honour and pride for a platoon commander to be able to say no member of his platoon developed 'Trench Feet' during the brigade's tour of duty in the frontline. Once daily the platoon commander will see that each NCO and man has 3 pairs of socks (1 in wear and 2 in kit) that boots are loosely laced, and when not actually on duty removed for a period, that puttees are not too tight, that when wet socks are taken off the feet are cleaned, dried and rubbed thoroughly with whale oil before dry socks are put on, that circulation is kept up by a few moments' occasional exercise, particularly after the men have been stationary while on duty, and that wet socks are collected and sent to company headquarters. (pp. 10–11)

Sandbagging is exhausting work even when working in a team but it is much easier to get earth into the bag in daylight than in the dark.

15:00

In preparation for the night-time work improving the trenches, some of the late afternoon is spent carrying out work that can be done without being seen by the enemy. This means filling sandbags and dumping them in position ready for dusk. It is important to ensure that this work is not in any way obvious to the enemy because if they suspect work will be conducted on a specific area that night it may well come under fire.

16:20

Half an hour before the sun goes down the men in the trenches must 'stand to' and will remain on alert for another half an hour after it is fully dark and the potential for a raid taking advantage of the low light levels has receded.

Notes for Headquarters of Battalions and Company Commanders on Trench Routine: 41st Division (February 1916) states:

> Half an hour before dark whole company will stand to arms, night positions will be occupied, bayonets fixed, and platoon sergeants will see that every man is able to fire over the parapet at the ground line of our wire (to do this it is not necessary to show the head above the parapet, but provided each man has a sufficiently high foot-rest to stand on, he will be able to fire over the parapet). Night sentries will be told off and posted. (p. 7)

One of the features of these twice-daily 'stand to's is that the sun comes up behind the majority of the German trenches on the Western Front and sets behind the Allied lines. This may not appear very important but for the soldiers it is a critical factor that must be taken into consideration. Every morning the Allied soldiers find themselves staring into the rising sun whilst at night they are silhouetted by the sun as it sets behind them. This is an ideal time for snipers to make the most of the situation and even without an attack 'stand to' has real dangers.

During 'stand to' the entire garrison of the trench must be ready to deal with an enemy attack. Bayonets are 'fixed' and the men start standing on the floor of the trench with the sentries watching through periscopes. As it becomes gradually darker the men are ordered to stand on the fire step slightly crouching and as it becomes fully dark to stand and to be fully erect with head and shoulder above the parapet. One reason for this is so they can see and hear the other is so that if an enemy soldier shoots at the top of the trench they will be hit in the shoulder or chest and not the head.

The men will stay in position waiting for the order to stand down for at least half an hour after last light. During this time no one can smoke, talk, or move about. Everyone is tense, waiting for a single shot or the noise of incoming artillery which is likely at this time of day. The enemy are doing the same thing at the same time and both sides are aware of the proximity of the other.

In the event of a raid, firepower is very important and the battalion's machine-gunners are distributed along the front to deal with the potential threat. To create the maximum damage the Lewis guns are positioned to shoot across the barbed wire defences so that an advancing enemy will walk into the line of fire.

The trench faces north-east in this area and the sun goes down behind their left shoulder, unlike almost anywhere else on the Western Front.

With bayonets fixed, the men watch their platoon commander who is observing no-man's-land through a periscope.

In the half light the men wait for the order to step up to the parapet and hope that the enemy cannot see them.

With a magazine of forty-seven bullets in position the Lewis 'automatic rifle' is ready. One of these weapons is more accurate and deadly than ten rifles.

17:30

As it is now fully dark the men can be ordered to 'stand down' but one in three will remain on guard duty for 1 hour at a time. This does not mean that the men can rest because night is the one period in which it is possible to repair the trenches, erect barbed wire or move in no-man's-land. Raids conducted by volunteers are rare but working parties are a nightly activity and there is no choice about participation.

With the order given to 'stand down' the men can step back from the parapet and night duties begin.

18:00

Supper

As it was too early to eat an evening meal before 'stand to' the men must wait until after this is completed before their supper. Due to the cold weather the men receive a second hot meal of soup and many add other items from their hoarded rations. As it is not possible to use torches, the men eat in the dark, opening tins largely by feel and accidents and mistakes are frequent.

Soldiers were rarely hungry but did find the rations monotonous and one side effect of eating so much protein was boils. These were a common problem and are frequently mentioned by younger soldiers who tended to overeat and not have any form of balanced diet. One way to provide variety was by buying pickles and sauces to flavour an otherwise rather bland and meaty diet.

Opening a tin of 'Colon' corned beef. Once opened it would have to be eaten very quickly as there is no safe way to store it and the rats were certain to discover any food source.

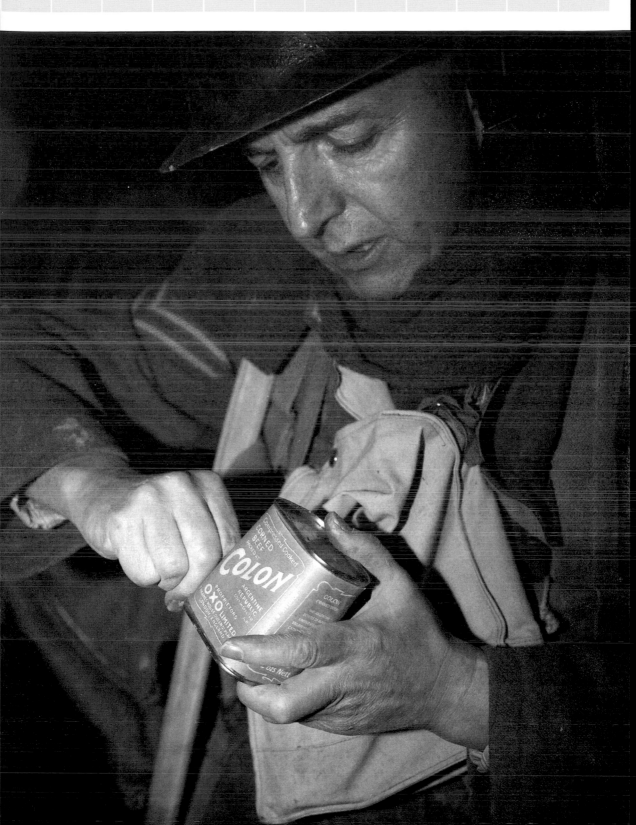

With the soldier on the right on guard duty another helps himself to the soup contained in the dixie standing on the fire step. The response from the men to someone clumsy enough to knock the rations over can be easily imagined.

A German flare drops in no-man's-land illuminating the men who are now 'standing to' and wearing respirators.

18:30

One aspect of trench warfare is the uncertain nature of every day. Soldiers know when they are going into attack or on a raid, they will be aware of when they are to receive leave or go on a course, but once in the frontline there is no way of telling what will happen next. Although there has been no enemy activity so far this does not mean that a jumpy sentry or accidental shot will not generate a full alert. At the time when it appears that the night-time routine is running as normal a British bombardment is commenced on the area of the German frontline to the west of Railway Wood. The German artillery cannot do anything other than respond in case this heralds an attack and within minutes a counter-bombardment begins to fall along the British frontline and in the rear area. Unfortunately further up the line a British gas sentry is convinced that he can smell gas drifting on the wind. Immediately the shout is given 'Gas! Gas! Gas!' and gongs and horns are sounded.

One reason for shouting 'Gas!' repeatedly was to expel any that had already been breathed into the lungs and also to warn others. Speed was essential and the helmet would be knocked off to hang, if you were fortunate, on your arm while the mask was fitted over the face and adjusted to ensure that it was not twisted and fitted tightly. With this in place a nose clip meant that the only way to breathe was directly through a rubber mouthpiece held between the teeth. Despite rubbing the eyepieces with soap or saliva these would tend to mist up quickly and it was very difficult to speak clearly with the respirator in place. Nonetheless if the men were confident that their respirator would work they could sit out most forms of gas attack.

With every man wearing his respirator they take up firing positions and wait to see what will happen next.

19:15

After half an hour and some more flares it is clear that no attack has developed. Despite the gas scare there is no proof that any was ever released and the garrison receives the order to 'stand down'. This kind of false alarm was far from uncommon but could not be ignored as the big attack could be just around the corner when everybody had relaxed.

With respirators back at the alert the men of the section discuss what has just happened before they are sent back to their duties, as this kind of congregating is an ideal way to suffer heavy casualties from enemy fire.

The first of two men scurry over the top as they head for a crater just short of the frontline. If German soldiers occupied this it would be very easy for them to throw grenades into the trench.

20:00

It was felt important to dominate no-man's-land and to do this meant raids, patrolling or putting parties of men into listening posts between the lines. This process was always dangerous as a crater that was empty on one evening could have been occupied by the next. If there was no 'sap' or trench to a forward position a detachment would be sent over the parapet with instructions to take over and improve a crater as an occupied position. The question was always would they be the first ones there?

By 1917 it was common practice to use both formal trenches and mine and shell craters as defences. Craters could be linked to each other or occupied singly and in this case minimum disturbance of the crater meant that it may not be spotted by aerial photographers. Although the men in the crater could shoot at attackers

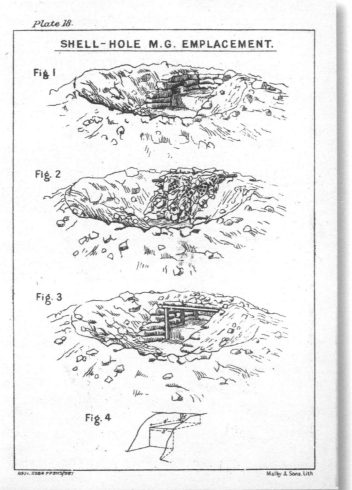

Diagram from the official manual showing how a shell hole should be improved for defence.

the information they could gain by remaining hidden and yet close to the enemy position was more important. Being in a forward position such as this for long periods was regarded as being especially taxing and the men would expect not to do this on a regular basis.

The normal way to 'improve' a crater was to dig a trench in the forward lip so that a standing soldier could shoot from behind cover. The earth removed could be loaded into sandbags and used to thicken the rim of the crater. In certain circumstances half of the front edge would be roofed over with boards covered in sandbags so that the little garrison could shelter underneath but fire from on top in the event of an attack.

With the first man in position the second follows bringing with him a telephone cable to communicate to the trench.

Whilst one man remains ready to fire the other digs and fills sandbags making minimum noise because they are so close to the enemy.

22:00 to 00:00

Braziers were issued to units and had to be signed for by an officer taking over a section of trenches. Using a combination of issued coke or charcoal together with fragments of boxes and other combustibles it was possible to light a warming but not too obvious fire.

Despite instructions to the contrary soldiers who were cold and wet would be quite prepared to take timber from their defences to burn, sacrificing long-term safety for short-term warmth. This was a constant problem and in the freezing conditions of 1917 a number of soldiers became so numbed by the cold that they committed suicide.

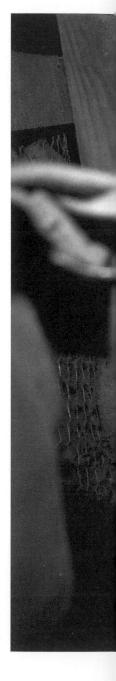

A soldier sits on the fire step with his feet on the parados to keep clear of the mud while a comrade huddles close to the brazier. Both men wait their turn on sentry duty.

Although officially discouraged as being both dangerous and wasteful the men would light fires to keep warm if they could get away with it. Here a hole has been cut in the traverse so that the glow from the fire cannot be seen from the enemy lines.

02:00

Most soldiers have had no more than 2 or 3 hours' sleep in the last 24 hours and are beginning to be exhausted. Although they are only on sentry duty at night for 1 hour at a time this is done every 3 hours and there is plenty to keep them busy in between. They alternate between working, resting and duty with little time to think other than when they are staring into no-man's-land.

04:00

During the day the main watches were around 4 hours long and during this time one officer and one NCO were on duty. From dusk till just before dawn the watches were no more than a couple of hours but during this time there would be an officer and NCO touring the trenches in case of problems and to ensure that the men were on duty and not sleeping or under cover and out of sight. It is important that this is done all night and it means that officers do not get better treatment than the men. Although torches were available most men worked by natural light simply because if they used bright lights then had to look into no-man's-land they would be night blind.

Although today people are aware of some soldiers being shot, having been found guilty of a military crime by a court martial, this represents a fraction of the number of men in service. In most cases the men were willing to carry out their duties because of a feeling of comradeship and respect for their officers. During an officer's watch he would visit sentries, see that they are alert, receive their reports and ensure that they are relieved on time. He would also supervise any work being carried out and ensure that the trench was clean and tidy.

The platoon commander turns the corner of a fire bay to check on its occupants.

A sentry shows how tired the men became, well aware of the
risks faced by dozing off for more than a few seconds.

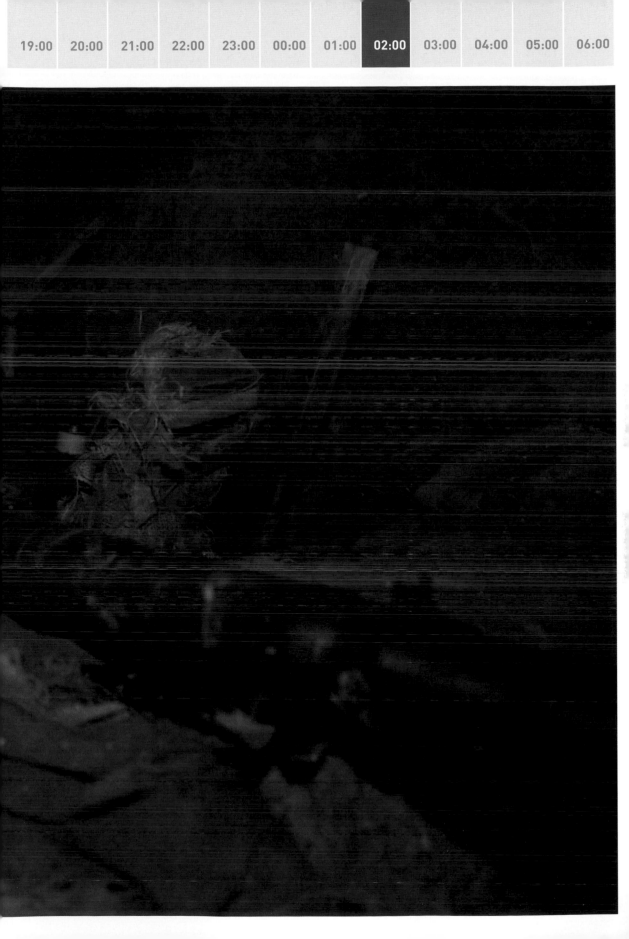

A tired sentry has a few words with the duty officer. Some words of encouragement could be as useful as an hour's sleep.

05:00 to 'Stand To'

The period before dawn is the coldest and darkest, and when the men are at their lowest. Some of the garrison manages to snatch some uncomfortable sleep whilst others remain on guard duty. A large number of cigarettes are consumed as people fight off fatigue and try to remain alert. With 'stand to' called for half an hour before first light it will be around 06:30 that the platoon commander will send word for everyone to move to their positions on the parapet.

Even the youngest and hardiest soldier is tested by the weather and exhaustion.

06:30

The routine of trench life means that everyone in the trench knows that they will be relieved by an incoming battalion that night. This will be their final evening in the trenches. Within 12 hours they can expect to be in dry, warm, comfortable billets deep in the ancient defences of the city of Ypres. They can congratulate themselves on having suffered relatively few casualties and even if they are not aware of inflicting any on the enemy they have taken another turn in the line. After a hot meal, a rest and an inspection to ensure that all kit is correct, at least some of them will be able to have a drink with their mates if they have not been chosen for guard duty or fatigues.

However, all that remains a few hours away and the arrival of the NCOs to get everyone on their feet, wide awake and looking towards an invisible enemy will be the next step in the day's routine.

****

This is a Tommy's life, not the glory of endless battle, nor the constant drain of mud, blood and bullets – it was the 24-hour questions of how to cook food, how to stay warm and how to relieve yourself, how to stay clean, and how to keep doing it day after day that should never be forgotten.

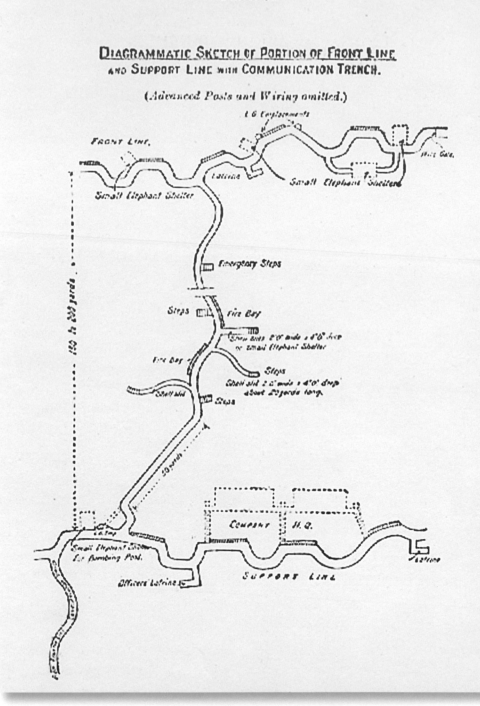

This illustration shows the relationship between the communication trench and the frontline with all the associated features. From: *Manual of Field Works (All Arms)*, 1921.

GLOSSARY OF TRENCH TERMINOLOGY

Batter	The angle of a trench wall away from the vertical.
Berm	A small ledge left between the parapet and the excavation of a trench.
Choke	The mouth of a sandbag when closed and tied off.
Command Trench	A trench constructed wholly or in part above ground level to avoid flooding.
Communication Trench	A trench linking one area of the trench system to another and not intended primarily for defence.
Dead Ground	An area that cannot be swept by a defender's fire.
Dugout	A shelter constructed below ground to give protection to occupants or stores.
Entanglement	Any obstacle, usually of barbed wire, designed to delay and channel an enemy's advance.
Field of Fire	An area of ground that is exposed to the fire of a body of troops.
Fire Trenches or Fire Bays	The foremost trenches occupied by the firing line.
Glacis	Gently sloping ground with little cover to the immediate front of the firing line.
Head cover	Protection for the heads of defenders when firing from a position.
Headers	The term applied to bricks, or in the case of trenches sandbags, laid at right angles to the face of the structure to serve as a bond.
Helve	The handle of a pickaxe or entrenching tool.
No-man's-land	The disputed area of ground between the opposing trenches.
Overhead Cover	Cover against projectiles which have a high angle of descent.
Parados	The rear face of a trench, from the French 'Cover Back'.
Parapet	The front face of a trench, from the French 'Cover Head'.
Recess	An opening made in the face of trench for the storage of ammunition or stores.
Revetment	Any method of making earth stand at a steeper slope than is natural. This can be stakes, corrugated iron, timbering or sandbags.

Sandbag	A hessian or canvas bag filled with earth, chalk, clay or occasionally sand, and used in fortifications.
Sap	A trench, which extends the line towards an enemy.
Splinter-proof	A shelter proof against small shell splinters or shrapnel.
Stretchers	The term applied to sandbags laid with their longest side parallel to the face of the structure.
Sump	An excavated drain in the floor or side of a trench.
Traverse	A bank of earth intended to give protection from flanking fire or to localise the effects of shells.
Trench	An excavation intended to provide cover or as a firing position.
Trench Board	A wooden mat or grating, sometimes called a 'duck board' designed to keep men's feet out of mud and water in addition to improving grip for users.

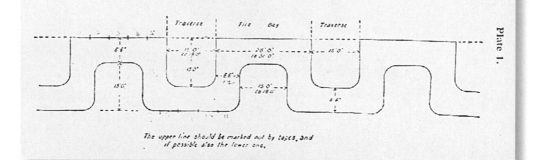

This diagram shows the theoretical layout of a fire trench and the use of traverses to divide up the fire bays. From: *Manual of Field Works (All Arms)*, 1921.

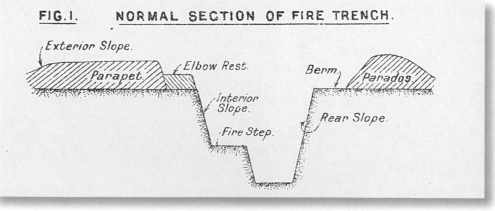

Diagram showing the relationship between the trench and the parapet and parados. From: *Manual of Field Works (All Arms)*, 1921.

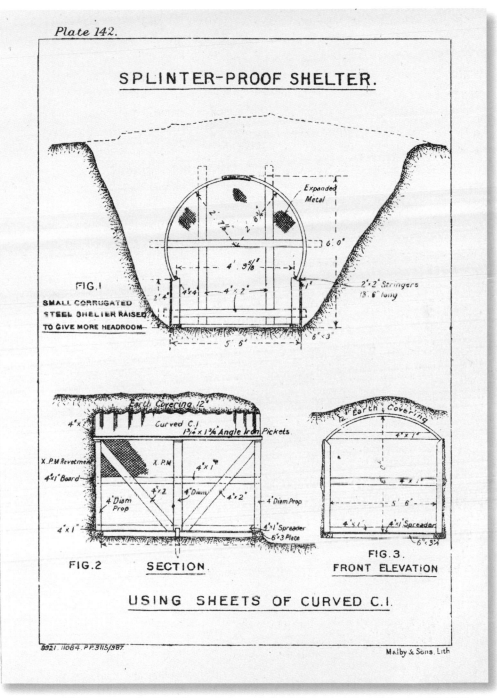

Plate 142.

SPLINTER-PROOF SHELTER.

FIG.1

SMALL CORRUGATED
STEEL SHELTER RAISED
TO GIVE MORE HEADROOM

Expanded Metal

6' 0"

4' 9⁵/₈"

2' 2" Stringers
13' 6" long

4"×4"

4"×2"

2' 4"

5' 6"

6"×3"

FIG.2   SECTION.

Earth Covering 12"

Curved C.I.

1¾"×1¾" Angle Iron Pickets

4"×

X.P.M Revetment

4"×1" Board

X.P.M

4"×1"

4 ' Diam Prop

4"×2

4" Diam

4"×2"

4' Diam Prop

4"×1"

4"×1" Spreader

6"×3 Plate

FIG.3.
FRONT ELEVATION

Earth Covering

4"×1"

5' 6"

4"×1"

4"×1" Spreader

6"×3"

USING SHEETS OF CURVED C.I.

8921. 11084. P.P.3115/987

Malby & Sons, Lith

This is an example of an infantry shelter as built for the project. From: *Manual of Field Works (All Arms)*, 1921.

An original 'A' Frame as excavated at Ypres.

FURTHER READING

Before Endeavours Fade, Rose E.B. Coombs, After the Battle, 2006.

Beneath Flanders Fields: The Tunnellers' War 1914–18, P. Barton, P. Doyle and J. Vandewalle, Spellmount, 2004.

British Uniforms and Equipment of the Great War, 1914–18, Vol. 1: Clothing and Necessaries, MLRS.

Liverpool Pals, G. Maddocks, Pen & Sword, 1999.

The Platoon: An Infantryman on the Western Front 1916–18, A. Robertshaw and S. Roberts, Pen & Sword, 2011.

The Story of the 55th (West Lancashire) Division, Rev. J.O. Coop, Liverpool, 1919.

The Third Ypres Passchendaele: The Day-By-Day Account, Chris McCarthy, Arms and Armour Press, 1995.

Tommy: The British Soldier on the Western Front 1914–18, Richard Holmes, Harper Collins, 2004.

Trench: A History of Trench Warfare on the Western Front, Stephen Bull, Osprey, 2010.

Undertones of War, E. Blunden, Penguin, 2000.

Official History

Military Operations. France and Belgium, 1917, Vol. 1, compiled by Brigadier General Sir James E. Edmonds, London, HMSO, 1940.

Military Operations. France and Belgium, 1917, Vol. 2, compiled by Brigadier General Sir James E. Edmonds, London, HMSO, 1948.

Training Manuals

Entrenching Made Easy, Temple Press, Undated.

Knowledge for War: Every Officer's Handbook For The Front, Capt. B.C. Harrison and Sons, Undated.

Infantry Training (4-Company Organization.), General Staff, War Office, HMSO, 1914.

Manual of Field Works (All Arms), HMSO, 1921.

Notes for Infantry Officers on Trench Warfare, HMSO, March 1916.

S.S.143 Instructions For the Training of Platoons For Offensive Action 1917, General Staff, February 1917.

S.S. 448 Method of Instruction in the Lewis Gun, General Staff, May 1917

The Pattern 1908 Web Infantry Equipment, War Office, 1913.

Trench Routine, 41st Division, HMSO, 1916.

24hr Trench: A Day in the Life of a Frontline Tommy

ABOUT THE PHOTOGRAPHER

PaGe Images is a father and daughter photography team consisting of Phil and Georgee Erswell.

Phil has been taking photographs for over thirty years both as a hobby and professionally. The professional side started after he was asked to photograph a friend's wedding twenty years ago. After that more requests started coming in and he was soon working as a part-time wedding and portrait photographer. On retiring from the Metropolitan Police after thirty years' service, he became a full-time professional photographer concentrating on events and weddings: 'Georgee and myself work well together. At weddings Georgee concentrates on the informal reportage portraits while I get on with the required shots. At events I take the images while Georgee sells & prints the images.'

When not working as a photographer Phil spends his time touring and researching the Great War, a passion that has developed over the last fifteen years. Some of Phil's images taken in France and Belgium can be seen on his other site at www.barbedwiretours.co.uk.

When I was contacted by Andy Robertshaw through Steve Roberts to photograph *24hr Trench* I jumped at the chance. I was combining two of my passions, photography and the Great War. The photography was a challenge as I wanted the images to look as authentic as possible but at the same time record everything Andy needed. Some of the images were taken from angles that would not have been possible in the trenches, from the parapet for example. However, the majority were taken from within the trench alongside the soldiers in the mud and water.

Although we were only there for 24 hours I started to appreciate the hardship and misery those guys must have gone through. And that was without being shot at!

Other titles published by The History Press

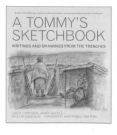

A Tommy's Sketchbook: Writings and Drawings from the Trenches

Lance-Corporal Henry Buckle, ed. David Read

During his time on the Ypres Salient Lance-Corporal Buckle kept a diary and sketchbook. He was a keen amateur photographer and water-colourist. Together with his diary, Henry Buckle's paintings, over sixty in number, provide a fascinating insight into life in and out of the trenches in France during 1915. Contemporary colour images from the front are all too rare, and Henry's charming and naïve pictures are full of exquisite details and insights.

978 0 7524 6605 7

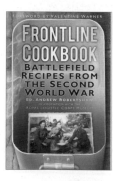

A Re-enactor's War: The Home Front Revisited and Remembered

John Leete

Mixing original period images with a selection of stunning colour images depicting the breadth of Second World War re-enactment, along with first-person accounts of re-enactment and their involvement with remembrance and the veterans, the reader will be fascinated by the characters, individual stories, amazing experiences and dedication.

978 0 7524 6603 3

Frontline Cookbook: Battlefield Recipes from the Second World War

Ed. Andrew Robertshaw

Frontline Cookbook brings together recipes from the Second World War, including hand-written notes from troops fighting in the Middle East, India and all over Europe. Many recipes are illustrated with cartoons and drawings on how to assemble the perfect oven and kitchen tools at a moment's notice from nothing. This book is the perfect inspiration for those who like to create an amazing meal anywhere, anytime, from anything.

978 0 7524 7665 0

A Bloody Picnic: Tommy's Humour, 1914–18

Alan Weeks

One of the crucial factors that kept Tommy going on the Western Front was his ability to see what was comic in the horror, deprivation and discomfort of trench warfare – an attitude which blossomed further in the rest areas behind the lines. And it wasn't only the British soldiers who managed to find something to laugh about in the trenches – the Germans could sometimes see the funny side as well. *A Bloody Picnic* presents an unusual perspective on how soldiers coped with the grim realities of the First World War.

978 0 7524 5668 3

Visit our website and discover thousands of other History Press books.

www.thehistorypress.co.uk